AHIMSA

By the same author

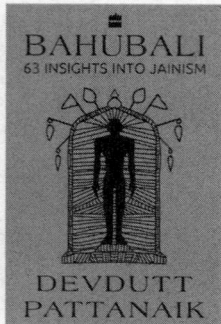

100 REFLECTIONS ON THE
HARAPPAN
CIVILIZATION

AHIMSA

WRITTEN AND ILLUSTRATED BY

DEVDUTT PATTANAIK

First published in India by
HarperCollins *Publishers* 2024
4th Floor, Tower A, Building No. 10, DLF CyberCity,
DLF Phase II, Gurugram, Haryana – 122002
www.harpercollins.co.in

2 4 6 8 10 9 7 5 3 1

Text and illustrations copyright © Devdutt Pattanaik 2024

P-ISBN: 978-93-6569-937-1

E-ISBN: 978-93-6569-903-6

The views and opinions expressed in this book are the author's own and the facts are as reported by him, and the publishers are not in any way liable for the same.

Devdutt Pattanaik asserts the moral right
to be identified as the author of this work.

All rights reserved. No part of this publication may be reproduced, stored in a retrieval system, or transmitted, in any form or by any means, electronic, mechanical, photocopying, recording or otherwise, without the prior permission of the publishers.

Typeset in Garamond by
Special Effects Graphics Design Co., Mumbai

Printed and bound at
Thomson Press (India) Ltd

This book is produced from independently certified FSC® paper
to ensure responsible forest management.

*To those who choose
dialogue (sam-vaad) and churning (manthan)
over
debate (vi-vaad) and submission (sharanam)*

Note on the Cover

The deep blue colour of the cover is that of lapis lazuli, a semi-precious stone found only in Afghanistan, that made its 5,000-kilometre journey to Sumer, in Mesopotamia, over 4,500 years ago, through the Harappan civilization, that thrived in the Indus river basin. Relative to most contemporary Bronze Age civilizations, Harappan cities showed a preference for non-violence (ahimsa), as indicated in a tiny seal (M-478B), creatively reimagined for the cover by the author.

Note on the Artwork

All illustrations are done by Devdutt Pattanaik. These are inspired, speculative and evocative, and not to be taken as 'real', or exact renditions. Geographical depictions are all schematic for easy understanding and not drawn to scale.

Contents

Introduction
1

Mythology
29

Resources
83

Knowledge
105

Standardization
159

People
201

Conclusion
239

Acknowledgements
251

Bibliography
253

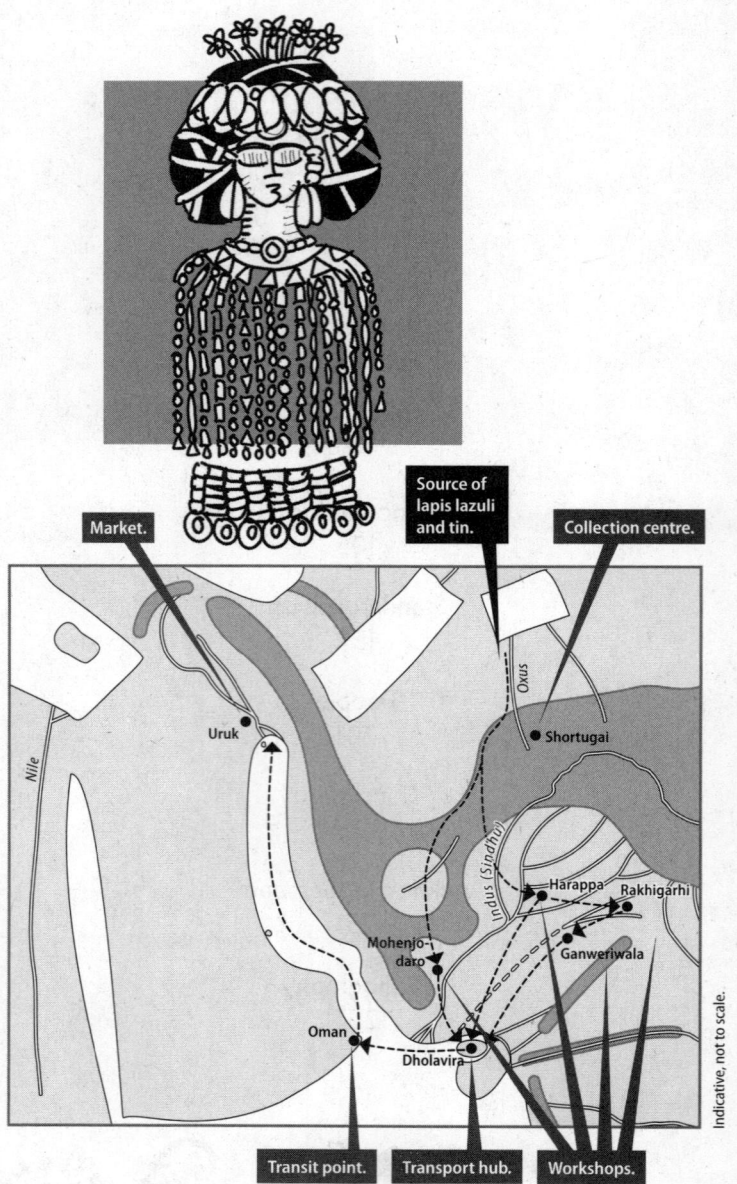

The supply chain of lapis lazuli.

INTRODUCTION
Non-Violence Is a Civilizational Option

Over 4,500 years ago, when the Egyptians were building pyramids, lapis lazuli, a deep blue stone, found only in Afghanistan, made a 5,000 km long journey, down the river Indus, up the Makran coast, and through the Persian gulf, to reach the temples of Mesopotamia, thanks to the Harappan civilization, a group of cities that followed a standard design and process template to create the world's first known supply chain. This was not an empire of warlords and kings. It was a creation of merchants, probably regulated by monks, who valorized restraint, and shunned vulgar displays of wealth. It was a unique civilization, industrial in scale, utilitarian in spirit, that chose stories rather than violence to get people to collaborate.

Constructing India's Past

Truth be told, we know about India's Harappan past only because of the British.

Before the British, this is what most Indians thought about the past:
- ▶ Since time immemorial, through four ages (chatur-yuga), Bharat or Jambudvipa (India), the land of seven rivers, had been ruled by kings and sages who descended from Manu, spoke Sanskrit, and followed sanatan (timeless) dharma, based of stratification of society (varna) and stages of life (ashrama), as prescribed by the Vedas.
- ▶ Everything changed when India was invaded by Yavanas (foreigners) who followed Turuku dharma (Islam), replaced temples with mosques, and Sanskrit with the Persian (Farsi) language.

But the British would change this traditional understanding of India's past.

The nineteenth century saw the setting up of the Asiatic Society that began translating ancient Indian texts, and the Archaeological Society of India that began unearthing various ancient artifacts. A new history of India emerged.
- ▶ Philological or linguistic studies revealed connections between Sanskrit and Latin and and led to the discovery of the Indo-European family of languages. Did it spread from India to Europe, or from Europe to India? The most likely location seemed to be somewhere in the middle.

- A new family of languages, the Dravidian family, was identified in India, thriving south of the Vindhya mountains, distinct from the Indo-European family of languages. Sanskrit was not the mother of all Indian languages, as claimed by Brahmins.
- Translations of Pali texts uncovered the Buddha, Ashoka and Alexander, who the Brahmins had forgotten. This was confirmed by the discovery of Buddhist stupas and Mauryan pillars and edicts. Objective evidence revealed that India's history began with the arrival of Alexander, 2,300 years ago. This rattled the Hindu orthodoxy.
- At this time, Max Mueller had completed his translation of the Rig Veda. He argued that the text was composed by a non-Semitic race from outside India, probably from the Caucasus, who called themselves Arya, around 1500 BC, and that it was as old as the Bible, if not older. By the turn of the century, Bal Gangadhar Tilak used astronomy-related hymns found in the Rig Veda to argue the text was composed much earlier, and farther away, when the sun was located in Taurus during the vernal equinox (4000 BC to 2000 BC), in a land closer to the Arctic regions, where there were dawns without sunrise. As these ideas provided an alternative to Semitic ideas (Judaism and Christianity) that dominated Western society, European racists were quick to appropriate the Aryan legacy.

Then, a hundred years ago, on 20 September 1924, the world learnt about the Indus (Harappan) civilization for the very first time. John Marshall, then Director General of the Archaeological Society of India, said this in the *Illustrated London News*.

> Not often has it been given to archaeologists, as it was given to Schliemann at Tiryns and Mycenae, or to Stein in the deserts of Turkestan, to light upon the remains of a long-forgotten civilization. It looks, however, at this moment, as if we are on the threshold of such a discovery in the plains of the Indus. ... Up to the present our knowledge of Indian antiquities has carried us back hardly further than the third century before Christ ... The two sites where these somewhat startling remains have been discovered are some 400 miles apart—the one being at Harappa in the Montgomery District of the Panjab, the other at Mohenjo-Daro in the Larkana District of Sindh. At both these places there is a vast expanse of artificial mounds evidently covering the remains of once-flourishing cities, which ... must have been in existence for many hundreds of years.

The dating was actually done through a 'Letter to the Editor' by Professor A.H. Sayce on 27 September 1924. He recognized the seals as identical to those he had found in Sumer, dated to 2300 BC. Thus India's history was objectively pushed back another 2,000 years. It all began 4,500 years ago, maybe 5,000.

Originally described as Indus-Sumerian, it was soon clear that this civilization had developed independently, and so was renamed Indus. But with sites found beyond Indus, in the mountains of Afghanistan in the west, the dry river bed of the Ghaggar-Hakra-Saraswati in the east, and the coast of Gujarat in the south, the civilization is now named after the first city discovered—Harappa.

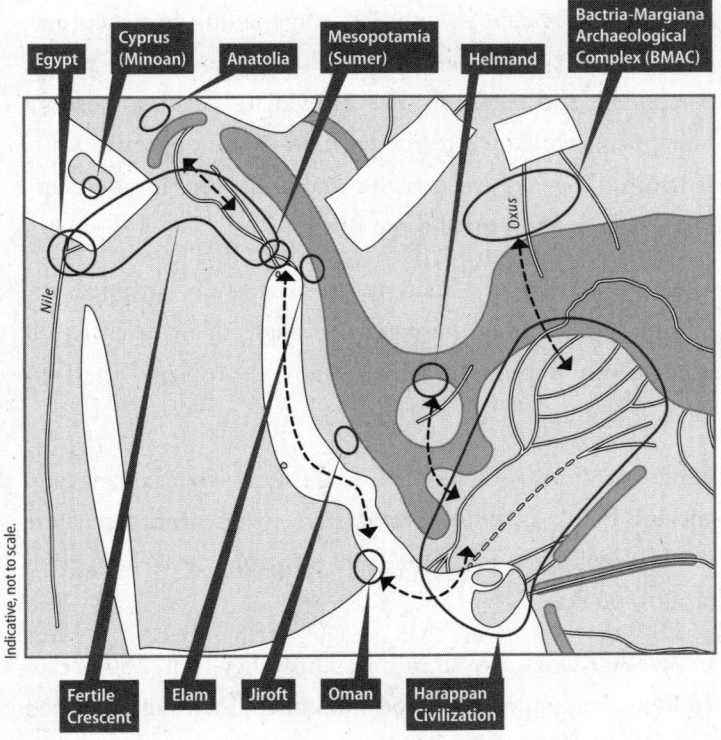

Ancient civilizations connected by the Bronze Age Trading Network (2500 BC).

There was no trace of Ram's kingdom, or the battleground where the Bhagavad Gita was revealed. Was the Harappan civilization Hindu? A cultural anxiety arose.

Based on their translations of the Pali and Sanskrit texts and of Ashokan edicts, the British had already established that Buddhism was non-violent, Hinduism was violent, and that the Brahmins did to Buddhists what the Muslims did to Brahmins later. The British then proceeded to interpret Vedic texts and the Harappan ruins in a way that justified their own colonization of India—the Sanskrit-speaking Vedic people conquered and enslaved the Dravidian-speaking peaceful Harappans, which led to the creation of the oppressive caste structure. They argued that the Brahmins were invaders too, just like later Muslims and the British!

This was a neat explanation. It successfully stripped the Hindu elite of moral outrage, and made them defensive. It became very popular. But there was one problem. The facts did not add up.

Now we know, thanks to linguistics, archaeology and ancient DNA analysis, that at least five centuries separate the Harappan period (2500-1900 BC) from the Vedic period (1500-500 BC).

Bronze Age cities thrived in the Indus valley from 2500 BC to 2000 BC, trading refined goods to Sumer. Their fall happened due to many reasons including climate change, shifting rivers, irregular monsoons, loss of exclusivity, rise of new trade routes

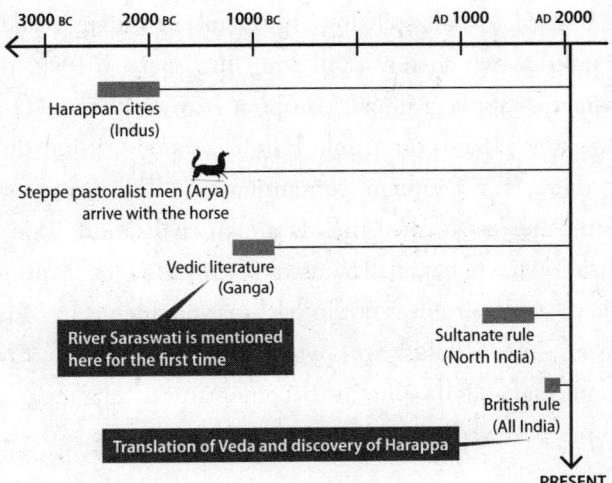

Timeline of Indian history.

(directly from the Bactria-Margiana Archaeological Complex, bypassing Indus) and decrease in demand (Sumerian culture being overwhelmed by the Akkadian empire).

There never was an Aryan invasion that caused the Harappan collapse. But there was an Aryan migration that took place centuries later. It involved men seeking to introduce horses and spoked-wheel chariots to a new market.

Many in India did not like, and still do not like, this new history.
- ▶ The Vedas could no longer be seen as the origin of all things Indian.
- ▶ Like the British, and the Mughals before them, the horse-riding Aryans, composers of the Vedas, were now established as outsiders.

This has led to hair-splitting arguments in Indian academia and politics, which now spill over into social media. There are theories about a global conspiracy to undermine Hindu civilization. That everything Hindu emerges from Indian soil; there is no foreign contamination. The Aryans were Indian. They established the Harappan civilization. That this civilization has to be called Saraswati civilization, reaffirming its Vedic roots. Its origin is not in Mehrgarh, which is in Muslim Pakistan, but in Rakhigarhi, which is in Hindu India. Ovens become yagna altars. Graffiti become yantras. Harappan diet becomes pure vegetarian, facts notwithstanding.

All this discomfort reveals how much our acceptance of the past is a function of the present. How big a role history plays in shaping our identity.

Bigoted Bards, Prejudiced Historians

We must keep in mind that subjects like the scientific study of language (philology) and historical objects, art and architecture (archaeology) began because Europeans were trying to prove the truth of the Bible. That the world began in 4004 BC, somewhere in Mesopotamia. But science upset such assumptions. Science argued the Vedic text was far older than the Bible. That Harappa was older than both. And even before Harappa there was Sumer, which told stories of the Great Flood, but had many gods.

Fact-based understanding of the past began only in the nineteenth century. Before that, history was the domain of bards. Bards are very different from historians.

- ▶ Bards seek to please their patrons with recitations glorifying the achievements of the dominant clan. So facts do not matter. Interpretation does. They are closed to changing their conclusions, and value 'faith' over 'scepticism'. They also find conspiracies everywhere. They are favoured by politicians as their narratives impact social change.
- ▶ Historians focus on facts first, and then present their interpretation. They are open to changing their interpretation when facts change or when their bias is pointed out. A good historian actively seeks more facts, as knowledge needs to expand. Politicians are wary of historians as the historian is committed to fact, not the political narrative.

That being said, historians are not rational, simply because they value facts. Facts do not speak for themselves. We need imagination to join the dots. This is especially true in social sciences (economics, politics, sociology, anthropology, history, psychology) relative to material sciences (physics, chemistry, biology). We can measure things; we cannot measure thoughts, emotions, feelings, dreams, fears. So prejudices always creep in.

- ▶ Orientalist historians were eager to show Harappa as a culture that was invaded and destroyed by chariot-riding Aryans, to justify their own colonization of India.
- ▶ Conservative Islamic historians are eager to show that Harappan cities were amongst those such as Aad and

Thamud, destroyed by Allah because they practiced idolatry, to justify the rise of Islam in Pakistan.
- Brahmin historians are eager to show Veda-chanting Aryans built Harappan cities on the banks of the river Saraswati, and even migrated westwards to civilize the world, to justify their dominant position in Hindu society.
- Jain historians are eager to show symbols of Tirthankar on seals to demonstrate their faith is timeless, and not merely a reaction to Vedic ritualism.
- Tamil historians are eager to show that Dravidians contributed to the building of Harappan cities because they know very well how Hindi-speakers of the north, who constitute 50 per cent of India's population, appropriate all things Hindu.
- Indian historians are eager to show that Harappan script is sound-based, just like Egyptian hieroglyphics and Mesopotamian cuneiform, and not meaning-based like an emoji or mathematical notation, because literacy has been traditionally equated with civilization.
- Communist and socialist historians see religion as an opium meant to control people, and are eager to find ancient egalitarian classless societies.
- Capitalist historians are eager to show how great civilizations can only be built by restless, ambitious and heroic leaders, who mobilize people to innovate, extract and exploit.
- Male historians see men as 'priest-kings' performing leadership roles while female figures become 'mother-

goddesses' and 'dancing-girls'. Queer artworks and figurines are simply ignored.
- ▶ Professional archaeologists are eager to keep every mystery alive to ensure funding does not stop. No one wants to tell a truth that is at odds with the global (Western?) discourse. No one wants to reveal a truth that can upset the local authority who can grant access to dig a site.

Different people have different truths. Even the objective of historians is influenced by the myth they live, the cultural truth they were exposed to since birth. Wars erupt when we try to impose one truth over other truths. Even though historians respect facts, their cultural bias seeps through in their interpretations. This is why academia is full of cantankerous debates, where every scholar has to defend their thesis, rather than simply explain their idea and assumptions.

The alternative is to listen to other truths and negotiate with multiple truths, a skill that ancient Harappans probably developed. For they worked with multiple merchant-guilds, spread across multiple cities, located in multiple geographies, and served multiple markets. This enabled them to be less violent, if not non-violent, and more accommodating of differences.

Shifting Focus from Raid to Trade

Colonial archaeologists were Christians. Their own imperial ambitions, as well as stories of the Old Testament, made them see the past in terms of invasions and conquests. Their feudal mindset is evident in words they used to describe the cities they discovered: citadel, bailey, lower town. They were not equipped to see Harappa as a merchant civilization regulated by monks, an idea familiar to Asians. Economy for them was extraction-based, not exchange-based. This mindset prevails even today.

Before the rise of temple-based Hinduism that depended on agricultural wealth, India's prosperity came from trading activities. Merchants favoured Buddhist and Jain monks. Monasteries, built on trade routes, enabled more trade, and even served as banks. Monks shunned iconography and all things permanent. One rarely sees archaeologists talk about this shravaka-shramana (householder-hermit) model when discussing Harappan cities. Harappa and Sumer were riverine civilizations connected by sea-coasts that used monsoon winds just like the maritime trading empires of Southeast Asia between AD 500 and AD 1500. It was easier and cheaper to transport goods using ships. There were no animals that had to be fed, no carts that had to be repaired.

The Harappan civilization did not exist in isolation. It was part of a vast global enterprise, the Bronze Age Trading Network, that existed between 3300 BC and 1200 BC, connecting:
- ▶ The agricultural communities on the banks of the Nile in Egypt, the Tigris and the Euphrates in Mesopotamia, and the Indus in India.
- ▶ The mining communities on the slopes of the Zagros, the Caucasus, the Hindu Kush and the Aravalli mountain ranges.

- The sea coasts of the Mediterranean Sea, the Persian Gulf, Makran and Gujarat.

The Harappan civilization marked the early stages of the Bronze Age Trading Network as well as the eastern edge of this trading network. It became highly organized from 2500 BC to 2000 BC (500 years) though some say for 700 years between 2500 BC and 1900 BC. During this period, it was probably the exclusive supplier of the rare blue stone known as lapis lazuli, and tin (a rare metal then) that turned copper into the much-in-demand alloy known as bronze.

- Both raw materials were obtained from present-day Afghanistan via the trading post of Shortugai close to the Oxus river basin.
- They were processed in sites located on banks of the river Indus.
- They were transported by boats from the Gujarat coast up the Makran coast to the site of Shortugai and then across the sea to Magan (present-day Oman), from where they made their way to Dilmun (present-day Bahrain), to Sumer (present-day Iraq), and further west to Egypt and north to Anatolia, in exchange for silver and gold.
- Lapis lazuli and bronze, like gold, were rare and so were seen as sacred materials, indicative of divine status, used in temples in Mesopotamia, Egypt, Anatolia and even the island of Crete.

Mythic Mindset

Earlier scholars thought that humans, after satisfying the 'real' needs of food and security, then indulged in 'fancy' ideas like religion, spirituality and faith. But now, it is clear that it is matters of faith i.e., mythology, that played a key role in the agricultural as well as the trading revolutions that shaped human history. Belief in gods and ideas of paradise motivates human groups to do intense labour, till the land, mine the earth, produce refined crafts and exchange them over long distances.

Egyptian art showing the violence of kings.

Sumerian art showing the violence of kings.

Indus art showing a woman stopping men from fighting.

Indus art showing a woman standing between two warriors.

Gods of Sumer sought bright cotton fabrics, fine beaded jewellery, timber, sesame oil, chicken, peacocks, dogs and water buffaloes from faraway Meluhha, the name they gave the Indus delta. In exchange they gave gold and silver (obtained from the northern hills of Zagros), fine woollen fabrics, maybe bitumen to waterproof the baths and bathing platforms of Harappan homes, and maybe Arabian incense to be burnt in perforated cylindrical pots.

Unlike the infamous East India Companies, that enabled Europeans to conquer and plunder Asia in the eighteenth and nineteenth centuries, Harappan traders did not use military might to gain access to markets. They also shunned vulgar displays of violence, and wealth used to intimidate people. In fact, they may have even created the world's first artwork depicting non-violence.

- ▶ In the 478B seal from Mohenjo-daro, in Sindh, a woman stands in between two men fighting with trees. Her hands are stretched out as she tries to separate them.
- ▶ In the K-65 cylinder seal from Kalibangan, in Rajasthan, which is over 600 km away from Mohenjo-daro, a woman stands in between two men, who are trying to spear each other. Both men try to grab the woman by her hand.

Archaeologists and art historians prefer to see these as images of two men fighting over a woman. The patriarchal gaze is hard to shed, even if you value science. Can an alternative exist?

Trading prevents hoarding as well as raiding. It creates an economy of mutual dependence, of debit and credit, of balance sheets that integrate people and communities and cities and cultures. Peace prevails as long as the accounting system is respected. These ideas still inform Buddhist, Jain and Hindu ideas of paap (debt), punya (credit), dharma (repaying debts) and moksha (freedom from both credit and debit). When did these ideas originate? Even before Harappan cities, even before agriculture, when humans learnt to count with their fingers and toes, as per anthropologists.

How Stories Shape Society

Archaeologists tend to be sceptical about the relatively peaceful nature of the Harappan cities, even though there is hardly any evidence of war within, or between, them. No sign of swords even. Of course, Harappans would have used some violence as a tool of political control, and to protect their precious goods from being stolen. Even 'democratic' Greek city-states had slaves! But the violence in Harappan cities was nothing on the scale of Egypt and Mesopotamia.

If not violence, how did the Harappan civilization get its people to align and obey? How was the high level of homogeneity achieved over a million square kilometres for 700 years? To find the answer, we need to closely observe parenting. Parents use violence, the threat of violence, or the promise of rewards, to get children to follow culturally acceptable behaviour. They also use stories to introduce social constructs that the child slowly assumes to be natural. Tribes, cultures and civilizations do the same—they use storytelling to get people to voluntarily domesticate themselves.

Every human needs a story to make sense of the world and of life. Culture provides that story, binding people together with a common vision. The word 'myth' refers to this cultural truth, and it comes from the Greek word 'mythos', which means 'stories that explain'. Stories are not rational. They appeal to human emotions, to our deepest insecurities and quest for meaning. Every culture has its own vision of the world that it transmits over generations using stories, symbols and rituals. In modern nation-states, they take the form of national myths that promote patriotism. Amongst revolutionaries, they take the form of imagined pasts full of injustice.

Egypt, Mesopotamia, India and China had different myths, hence unique identities, which manifested in different kinds of art of architecture. Archaeologists nowadays prefer to use the word 'ideology' rather than 'mythology', making it sound rather rational and intellectual, stripping it of its primal irrational nature, rooted in human cravings and terrors. Those who wish to understand Harappan ideology need to first admit and appreciate their own irrational myths—something academicians rarely do.

Postmodern activists, who oppose such 'brainwashing' social constructs, end up creating their own myths for their own tribes, threatening those who oppose them with cancel culture. There is no escaping myth. It is the operating system of societies. It creates values, beliefs and customs that seem rational to the in-group (halal-haram binary of Islam, bushido code of Japan) but not by the out-group. Without myth, we are lone animals without a herd, hive or pack.

So what was the Harappan story? Here is a proposition. It was a merchant-monastic ecosystem like Jain, Buddhist and Hindu orders of later times, where material power was aquired through wealth and success while moral power was obtained by giving up wealth, relationships and trappings of success.

Unicorns as Hermit-regulators

Sumerian mythology spoke of gods who created humans to do the labour so they lived in luxury. Egyptian mythology spoke of the pharaoh who lived in the intersection of gods, humans and ancestors, and through whose body divine favour could be extracted. Power was needed to get people to give the gods what they desired (in Sumer) and to enchant the distant gods (in Egypt).

In both cultures, power was acquired by hoarding wealth. But in Harappan myth, power was probably acquired by renouncing wealth. This explains why the elite of Harappan civilization shunned every cultural tool of intimidation (monumental art, grand palaces, elaborate tombs) and embraced a rather stark architectural style, shorn of ornamentation. Ancient

Mehrgarh in Balochistan had colourful pottery. Dholavira in its early phases had brightly painted white and pink fortress walls. This colourful phase ended as soon as the Harappan urban phase of standardized weights, dominated by unicorn seals, came into the picture.

It is possible that the entire civilization was administered by hermit-regulators. These hermits most probably came from merchant backgrounds—for they clearly valued trading over raiding.

- ▶ Hermits who come from warrior backgrounds reject violence, valorize generosity, and generally shun social commitments.
- ▶ Hermits who come from merchant backgrounds do not seek solitude. They seek conquest of the mind. They warn against greed, hoarding and trickery. They know how markets run with rhythmic regularity, and so they establish worldviews based on debit, credit and balance of payments.

Moral authority, and legitimacy, is obtained only when a successful merchant gives up his assets, his relationships, his status and even his gender. Respect thus earned is used as currency to institute and maintain an elaborate faith-based system that restrains creativity and individualism, promotes standardization, enables collaboration, facilitates commerce and minimizes conflict, without compromising on the importance of family and clan. They were probably represented by the unicorn, which appears on 80 per cent of the seals found in Harappan cities, and whose disappearance coincides with the end of the civilization.

The word 'unicorn' comes from a mistranslation of a Hebrew word in the Bible meaning auroch, a now extinct giant bovine. It was seen as a divine creature that in later Christian art was linked to innocence and purity, and was drawn to maidens. It was visualized as a horse-like creature but in Harappan art the creature is more cow-like or antelope-like, like a one-horned nilgai, or a one-horned bison. This creature, widely represented, more than any other creature,

Harappan unicorn figurine.

Harappan unicorn seal.

Christian unicorn.

Chinese unicorn (Xiezhi).

and even represented in figurines, stands apart from two-horned virile animals such as the goat, bison, buffalo, bull, and even 'horned' tigers and elephants, which were probably mascots of merchant guilds.

This proposition is not as fantastic as it sounds. The power of the hermit in contemporary India needs to be seen to be believed. What follows is a paraphrased version of the Khaggavisana Sutta, from the earliest layers of the Buddhist canon. Khaggavisana means a sword-like horn, which is commonly taken to mean the solitary one-horned rhinoceros. However, it could as well refer to some kind of mythical unicorn. For the unicorn is not a natural beast, and is better suited for representing self-restraint, celibacy and continence, which are not natural states.

> Wander alone like a unicorn!
> Renouncing violence, children and companions,
> wander alone like a unicorn!
> Reject longing, shun adornment, speak the truth.
> Wander alone like a unicorn!
> Abandon family, riches, grain & pleasure.
> Wander alone like a unicorn!
> Like a fish in the water tearing a net, like a fire not
> coming back to what's burnt.
> Wander alone like a unicorn!
> Eyes downcast, not footloose, senses guarded, with
> protected mind, not oozing or burning with lust.
> Wander alone like a unicorn!

India has a long history of merchant-monastic (shravaka-shramana) ecosystems.

- ▶ Buddhist monasteries across Asia were established along trade routes and served as resthouses, warehouses and banking establishments.
- ▶ Jain temples housing images of naked ascetics were always built near markets, reminding the successful that true success was conquering hunger, not hoarding food.
- ▶ Hindu temple complexes run by hermit-managers (retired householders) use recurring agricultural income to promote refined arts and crafts through a set of highly dramatic congregational, seasonal rituals, where every community had a role to play.
- ▶ Across India, cattle trade fairs are held on religious occasions. There were trade fairs held in coasts to welcome ships from the Middle East and Southeast Asia that sailed in annually with the monsoon winds.

In the tenth century, the Christian Knights Templar learnt the secret of banking and promissory notes from Arab traders, who had been trading with Indians since Harappan times. But unlike old Indian bankers, the Knights Templar were also ruthless warriors, who did not know the spiritual secrets of 'writing off debts' and 'letting go', which is why the Christian, Jewish, and later Islamic banking systems faced such opposition in Middle Eastern and European cultures.

There is even a Chinese folktale from the Han period (200 BC to AD 200, the time of the Satavahana kings of India), that speaks of an ox-like unicorn, Xeizhi, an androgynous creature that came from a faraway land (Indus?) and was capable of identifying and impaling criminals. It became an icon of anti-corruption imperial officers. Could this have been the role of the Harappan hermit-regulators?

Of course, all these examples are less than 2,500 years old. But it is not impossible that someone had similar ideas 4,500 years earlier. If we can imagine bloodthirsty and tyrannical colonizers in ancient times, why can we not imagine non-violent merchant-mendicants? Buddhist and Jain scriptures insist that there were Buddhas and Tirthankaras who lived long before the historical Buddha and the historical Mahavir.

The absence of war, however, does not mean absence of oppression. The hermit can be as manipulative as a warlord can be violent. Puritanism gives rise to notions of purity and pollution, isolation of castes, and draconian practices like untouchability. Survival depends on restraint and balance. Sometimes, the best systems snap. Naturally, the Harappan way could not last forever. When the markets collapsed, when prosperity was in jeopardy, the monastic demand of patience, restraint and discipline may also have lost its glamour, resulting in the crumbling of the order.

The Harappan civilization did end rather abruptly around 1900 BC. It was marked by the sudden disappearance of the unicorn seal. This end was non-violent though, a gradual erosion of the regulated urban economy. The same cannot be said of the Bronze Age collapse that occurred rather brutally on the western edge of the trading network in 1200 BC. But that is another story.

Mythology Underlying History

History is shaped not by facts or rational thought. It is shaped by beliefs, by myths, by emotions. In the nineteenth century, myth was equated with falsehood. Truth was based on facts, not faith. The material and the measurable were privileged as 'real'.

In the twenty-first century, it is clear binaries do not explain human conduct. For human emotions, and imagination, defy measurement.

- ▶ Fact is everybody's truth based on measurement.
- ▶ Fiction is nobody's truth based on fantasy.
- ▶ Myth is somebody's truth based on faith.

Harappa had its own truth, which shaped its art and architecture, its customs and beliefs. Every historian and archaeologist has his or her own truth, which manifests in how they interpret Harappan truths. Harappans did not conduct their lives rationally. Just as historians tend not to interpret the past objectively.

We need to admit that modern history was invented by Europeans who were Christians, who therefore saw history as prelude (like the Old Testament) to a grand climax—the scientific equivalent to the Second Coming of Jesus. That is why, even today, many historians believe it is their job to unravel past wrongs in the pursuit of social justice. The past is therefore always seen in terms of the elite and the oppressed. The historian then positions himself or herself as a prophet, who warns people of doom if they repeat past mistakes.

There are other ways to look at the past, without being burdened by the notion of justice, a monotheistic myth of Middle Eastern origin. We can approach it philosophically. Study it to see what makes us human. How do we mobilize people to domesticate nature and extract wealth, power and meaning?

- ▶ The presence of fantastic beasts like the unicorn, the bull-man and the tiger-sphinx on Harappan seals are indicative of the human ability to be creative and look beyond the mundane.
- ▶ The obsession with symmetry, modularity, uniformity and functionality, in both art and architecture, reveals a love for efficiency, fear of unpredictability, and the need for control.

The past can easily guide us to make better sense of our present. Hence, this book.

This book is also an homage to a great civilization of peace that rose and fell over forty centuries ago, but was discovered only a century ago. Unlike the Vedas, which are full of sounds, rhythms, words and stories, the Harappan cities are silent, revealing their secrets through tantalizing visuals—a few seals, a few artifacts and a vast architectural blueprint. How did the Harappans imagine the world? I am eager to know.

What I present is not the truth. It is my truth, informed by thirty years of decoding stories, symbols and rituals. In these years, I have spotlighted the difference between one-life myths (which inform academia, modern management and Western societies) and rebirth myths (that shape India). I have highlighted how modern nation-states are driven by Greek ideas of a violent hero, and Christian ideas of tribal prophets leading nations towards Promised Lands. Most historians show little interest in Jain, Buddhist and Hindu ideas of life as a network of interdependent balance sheets. These models are therefore not factored in when we study Harappan art and architecture. Without an underlying mythology, Harappan material culture seems like a sterile set of facts about zombie traders.

In this book, I reflect on:
1. Harappan mythology, which reveals their imagination.
2. Harappan resources, which reveals their geography.
3. Harappan knowledge, which reveals their economics.
4. Harappan homogenization, which reveals their politics.
5. Harappan people, revealing their humanity.

I wish to demonstrate how Indians have always balanced materialism with monasticism, resisted empires, and grown weary of systems of standardization, always preferring diversity and autonomy.

What I present are not arguments. These are reflections, based on frameworks that I have developed to better understand various Indian and world mythologies. These are not free of my prejudices. So approach this book in the spirit of curiosity, not combat. Allow your mind to expand, guided by the following lines:

> *Within infinite myths lies an eternal truth.*
> *Who sees it all?*
> *Varuna has a thousand eyes*
> *Indra, a hundred*
> *You and I only two.*

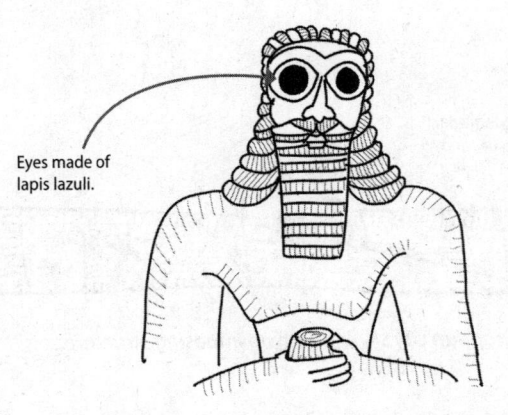

Eyes made of lapis lazuli.

Sumerian image of a devotee before a deity.

Sumerian city skyline dominated by a temple.

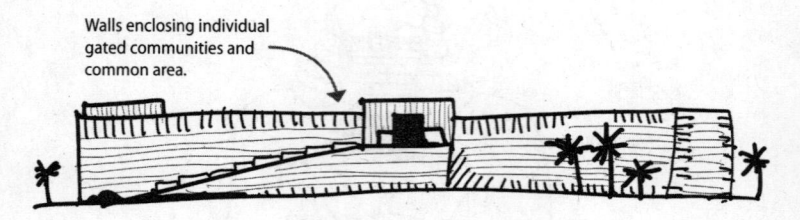

(label: Ziggurat, home of the gods.)

Harappan city skyline with no imposing structure.

(label: Walls enclosing individual gated communities and common area.)

Mythology

Myths give meaning. They bind people and mobilize them. Sumerian myths mobilized people to work together, build canals, establish farms, take care of livestock and provide for the city-gods, who could otherwise cause floods and disease. Harappan myths were for urban folk, not farmers, or herdsmen. They were designed to get secretive and competitive clans to collaborate with each other and establish an efficient trade network, based on purity, avoiding monumental art and architecture designed to intimidate.

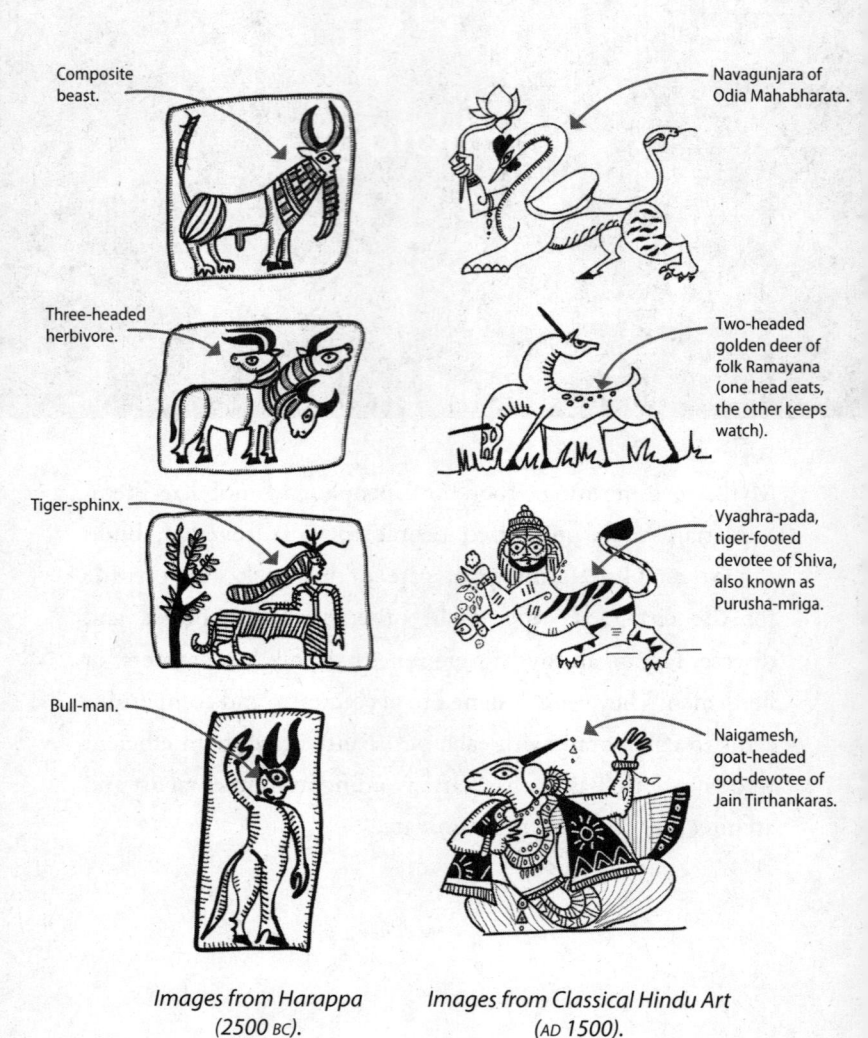

Composite beast.

Navagunjara of Odia Mahabharata.

Three-headed herbivore.

Two-headed golden deer of folk Ramayana (one head eats, the other keeps watch).

Tiger-sphinx.

Vyaghra-pada, tiger-footed devotee of Shiva, also known as Purusha-mriga.

Bull-man.

Naigamesh, goat-headed god-devotee of Jain Tirthankaras.

Images from Harappa (2500 BC).

Images from Classical Hindu Art (AD 1500).

1. Fantastic Beasts

The key indicator of imaginative mythic thinking in a culture is the appearance of fantastic beasts—creatures that do not exist in nature: goat-headed fish, flying bulls, human-headed serpents, bird-headed lions. Such art first appears on cave walls nearly 40,000 years ago. Archaeologists have noticed a sudden spurt of such art within the Bronze Age Trading Network as more and more people were exposed to strange foreign cultures, and the rise of urban ecosystems, where work and life became more industrial, more mechanical, and less driven by natural rhythms.

Harappan cities were no exception, with many fantastic beasts depicted on seals and clay tablets.
- ▶ Bull-men.
- ▶ Tiger-goddesses.
- ▶ Unicorn with a bovine body.
- ▶ A herbivore with three heads of different species.
- ▶ A composite of seven beasts.

Many of the fantastic beasts are still found in Indian lore. Are these remnants of Harappan memories? We can only speculate.

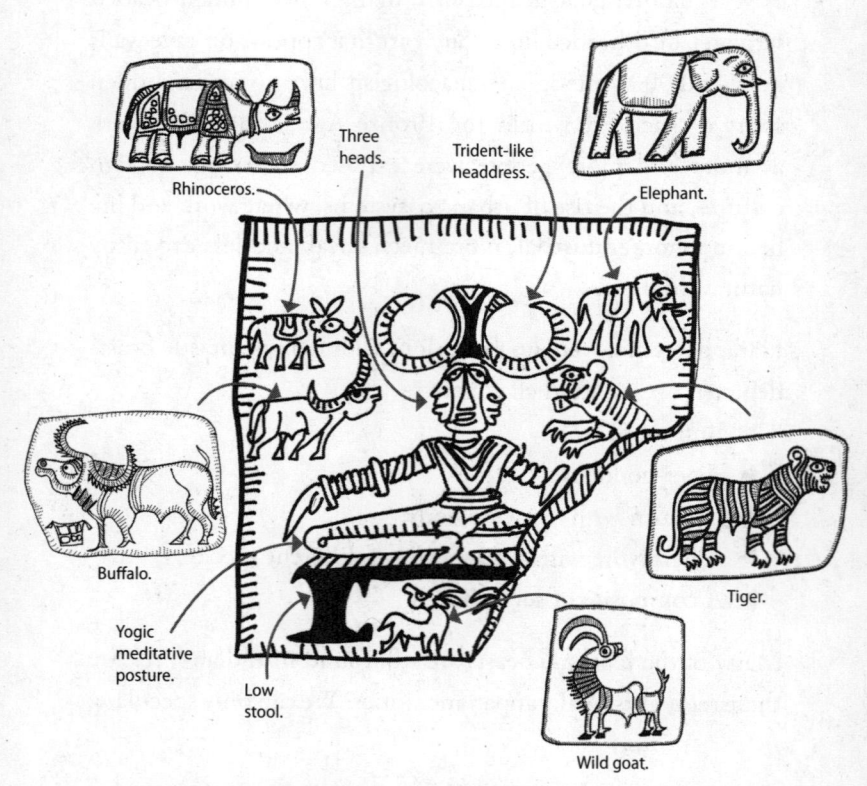

The Pashupati Seal brings together animals found on other seals.

32   *Ahimsa*

2. Not Quite Shiva

A hundred years ago, British archaeologists found a Harappan seal with the image of a horned being surrounded by wild animals. They identified it as Pashupati: Shiva, the beast-master.

Classical Shiva images appeared only 2,000 years later. In these images, Shiva is never shown wearing horns. As Gajantaka, he flays elephants alive. As Vrishabha-nath, he rides bulls. His consort, Shakti, rides tigers and kills buffalo-demons.

In the Vedic texts, the Shiva-like Rudra is a protector of cattle from wild beasts. Art historians have argued that the 'three heads' are probably a misreading of the dewlap of a bull's head, severed and placed over a priest-shaman's head. Images like this have been found in Elam culture of coastal Iran. Also, the image need not be male.

More importantly, the 'wild' animals are exactly the same animals found in stamp seals, so mascots of merchant guilds, making this more likely a marker of a meeting of competitive clans in a collaborative exercise.

We see what we want to see.

Shreyans-nath's symbol (Rhinoceros).

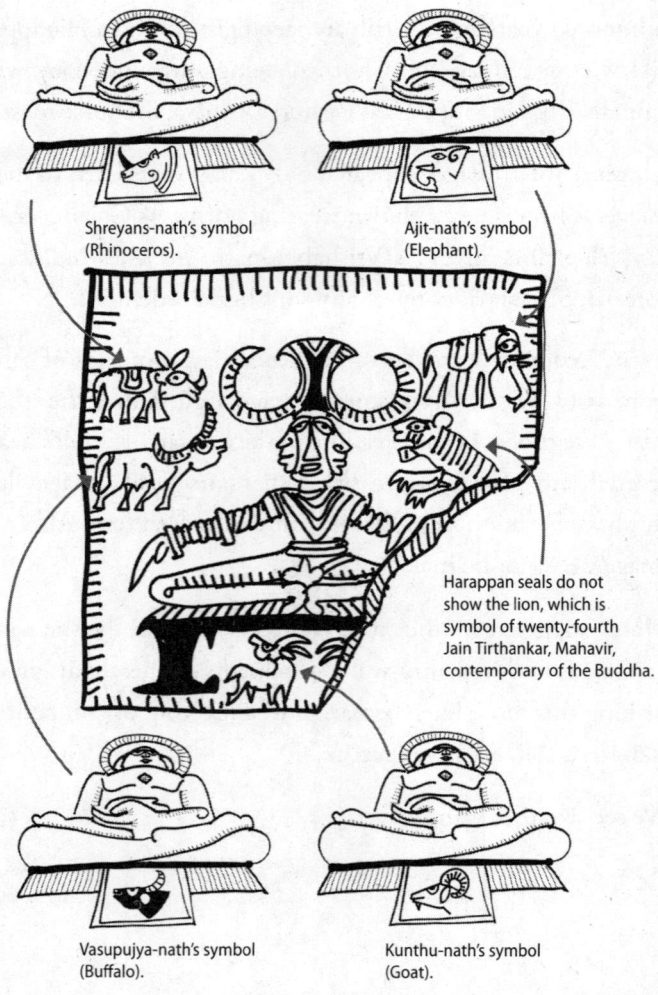

Ajit-nath's symbol (Elephant).

Harappan seals do not show the lion, which is symbol of twenty-fourth Jain Tirthankar, Mahavir, contemporary of the Buddha.

Vasupujya-nath's symbol (Buffalo).

Kunthu-nath's symbol (Goat).

Images on Harappan seals reappear as symbols of Jain Tirthankars.

3. Clan Animals, Caste Gods

The pashu (beasts) of the Pashupati (beast-master) seal are all wild: the rhinoceros, the elephant, the buffalo, the tiger, the mountain goat. All except the tiger have become symbols of Jain Tirthankars or turn into gods in the subaltern (desi) Hindu traditions.

- ▶ The buffalo becomes Mhaso-ba, form of Shiva, also Mahisha, the enemy of the Goddess who impales him.
- ▶ The tiger becomes Vagho-ba, form of Shiva, who the Goddess rides.
- ▶ The bull becomes Basava, form of Shiva.
- ▶ The goat head replaces the head of Daksha, beheaded by Shiva.
- ▶ The elephant head replaces head of Vinakaya, also beheaded by Shiva.
- ▶ The rhino (ganda) becomes the food to be offered by kings to ancestors.

As they are also found in stamp seals that were possibly used by merchant guilds who lived in gated communities of Harappan cities, these could have been the primal clan gods (kula-devata).

A kula could be found in many cities and towns, and they were bound by marriage and trade. Were these proto-castes (jati) long before they were categorized as varna in Vedic texts?

Man with monkey imported from the Indus region.

Harappan script.

Falaika seals

Indicative, not to scale.

Clay figurine of monkey from Harappa.

People of Sumer believed that Dilmun in the east was paradise.

Ahimsa

4. Religion of Trade

We easily accept the idea that religions propel violence—Christianity wiping out the Aztecs and Incas in the Americas, Islam wiping out Zoroastrianism in Persia. We resist the idea of religions promoting non-violence through trade. Harappan cities rose primarily to satisfy the Sumerian demand for ritual goods.

- ▶ Sumerians believed that gods created humans to be their servants and provide them luxuries such as cotton, tin, lapis lazuli, even exotic pets like monkeys, peacocks and roosters, from faraway lands: Dilmun (Kuwait, Falaika island, Bahrain), Magan (Oman), and Meluhha (Makran).
- ▶ The Sumerian goddess Inanna established trade between the city of Uruk in Mesopotamia, a source of grain, and the mountain lands of Aratta, a source of stones and metal. The mountain people were impressed with King Enmerkar used 'writing' to transmit long messages that no one could remember.
- ▶ Dilmun in the east was considered paradise by the Sumerians—a land where there were no predators and where no one grew old. The land through which came lapis lazuli and tin.

Deep blue lapis lazuli came from Afghanistan.

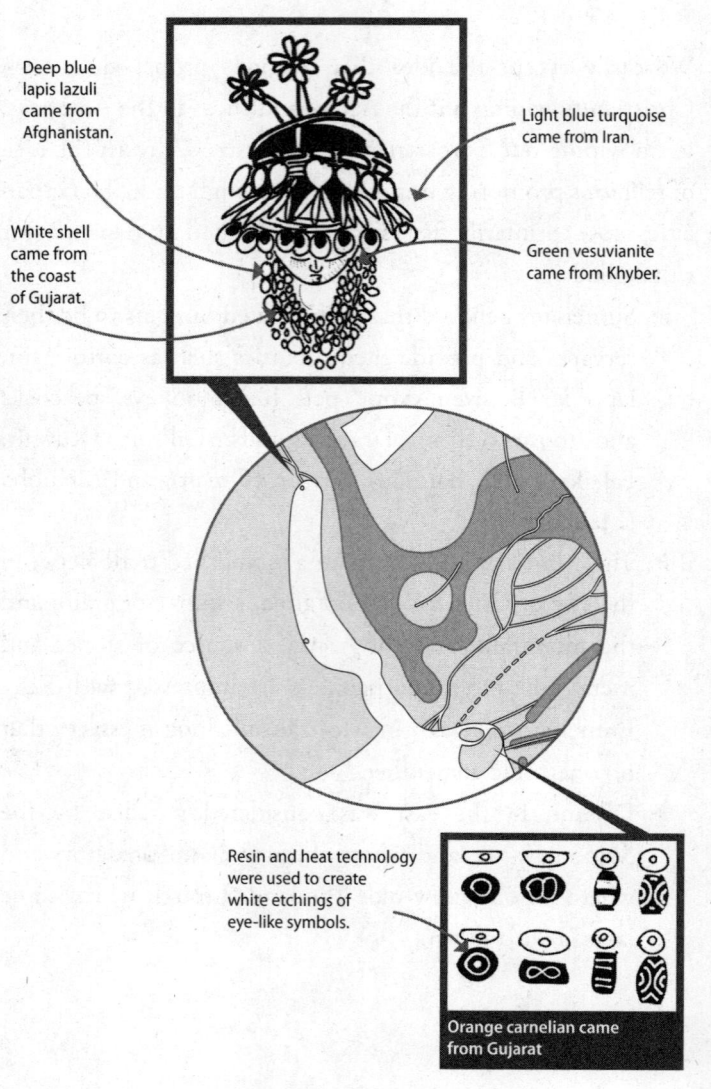

Light blue turquoise came from Iran.

White shell came from the coast of Gujarat.

Green vesuvianite came from Khyber.

Resin and heat technology were used to create white etchings of eye-like symbols.

Orange carnelian came from Gujarat

Indicative, not to scale.

Sumerian luxury goods.

Ahimsa

5. Occult Solutions from Harappa

Since historians value science, they value the rational side of cultures—the technological advancements.

But the humans who create culture are not just rational folks with engineering skills. They are emotional—with fears and insecurities, and belief in gods, ghosts and demons. Because of this, they require all kinds of 'irrational' material artifacts to cope with their 'irrational' yearnings and terrors.

- ▶ Cuneiform tablets from Sumer contain information on spells and incantations about demonic and helpful spirits. The semi-precious stones exported by Harappan cities served as talismans and charms sought by astrologers and other occult experts. The symbols and designs used on cloth and clay were magical signs to attract good luck and ward away danger.
- ▶ In Sumerian mythology, when the goddess Inanna went to the underworld to look for her lover Dumuzi, she was stripped of her clothes and jewellery and so was trapped there in naked poverty, until she was rescued by an androgynous being. So clothes and jewellery, blessed by sacred marks made by androgynous beings, were linked to protection from otherworldly forces.
- ▶ Fortune and fertility indicated divine grace. Misery and poverty indicated the anger of gods or demonic affliction.

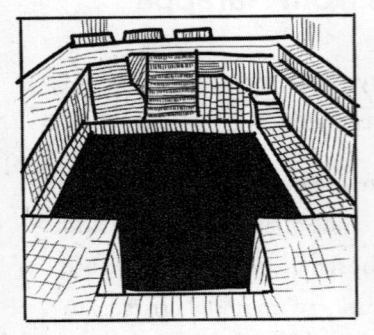

Great Bath of Mohenjo-daro.

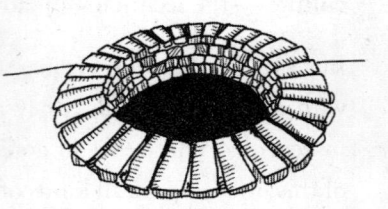

One of 700 wells of Mohenjo-daro.

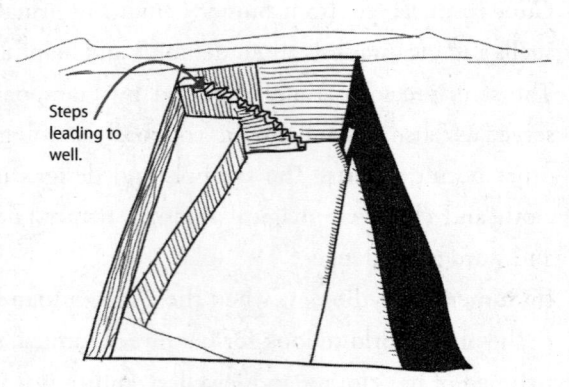

Steps leading to well.

Rock-cut reservoir of Dholavira.

Impure enter.

Leave purified.

Water resources across Harappan cities.

6. Purity and Sacredness

The stones that came from Meluhha were special—they were pure, held only by the hands of artisans who washed themselves regularly and lived in isolated workshops, avoiding contact with polluted folk. The beads and bangles were sealed in pots until they reached Sumer. This belief alone explains the Harappan obsession with gated communities, isolated courtyards without street-facing windows, bitumen-lined bathrooms, indoor lavatories, with soak-pits, storm sewers to prevent flooding of streets and elaborate drainage systems with terracotta pipes. These cities stood as long as demand lasted.

The urban isolated life behind gated compounds was not for all Harappans. It was only for those involved in the manufacture and supply of special ritual goods. Secular minds think of these as luxury and prestige goods.

Those who appreciate the value of the sacred, know the power of ritual goods. Jade, for example, is sacred to the Chinese but not Hindus. Hindus revere Rudraksha beads from trees that grow in Nepal, and Shaligram stone (ammonite fossil) found in Gandak river. These have no intrinsic material value.

Fish-eye.

Fish.

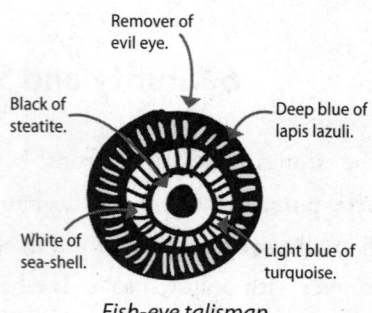

Remover of evil eye.

Black of steatite.

Deep blue of lapis lazuli.

White of sea-shell.

Light blue of turquoise.

Fish-eye talisman.
Inlay work of Harappan craftsmen.

Demons tormented Inanna, goddess of prosperity and luxury, until she was rescued by androgynous creatures created by Enki, god of water.

Tormenting those who do not have the protection of gods.

Sumerian seal showing 'galla' demons.

On head.

On arm.

Protective jewellery.

Ahimsa

7. Nazar or Evil Eye

Even today, from West Asia to South Asia, across the Middle East, people believe in 'nazar' or the evil eye. When this strikes, people become weak, tired, dehydrated and listless. It is linked with aridity. To counter it, one needs moisture—and salt, which retains moisture. So the talisman used even today to protect people from the evil eye is a fish-eye shaped amulet, ringed with white and blue.

Fish, with their unblinking eyes in constant contact with water, may have inspired the design. The many types of fish symbols used in Harappan script may be lined to these beads used to make fish-eye amulets.

The fish-eye amulet is seen on the head and the arm of the 'priest-king', an inlay work of Harappan craftsmen. The location on the head makes one wonder if Harappans believed in the 'third eye'. Those who practice aura therapy today believe lapis lazuli is for the third-eye chakra, turquoise for the throat-chakra, and carnelian for the solar plexus. It is not impossible that ancient Sumerians and Harappans had similar beliefs.

Sumerian mythology speaks of terrifying 'galla' demons of the underworld who experience no pleasure and derive nourishment from other people's pain. Even gods needed spells to protect themselves.

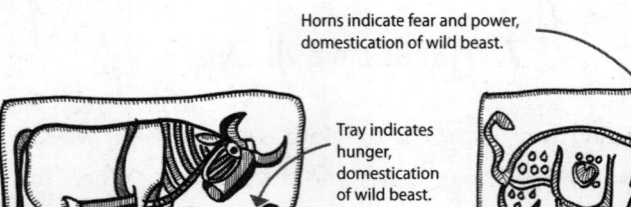

Horns indicate fear and power, domestication of wild beast.

Tray indicates hunger, domestication of wild beast.

A bison with tray.

'Horned' elephant.

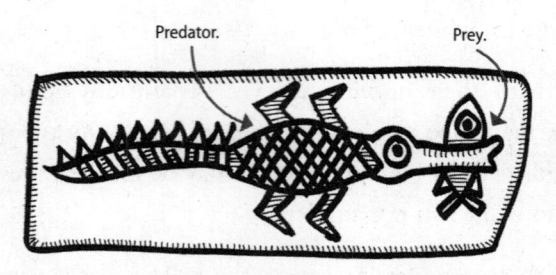

Predator.

Prey.

Jungle Law known in Sanskrit as Matsya Nyaya (Fish Justice).

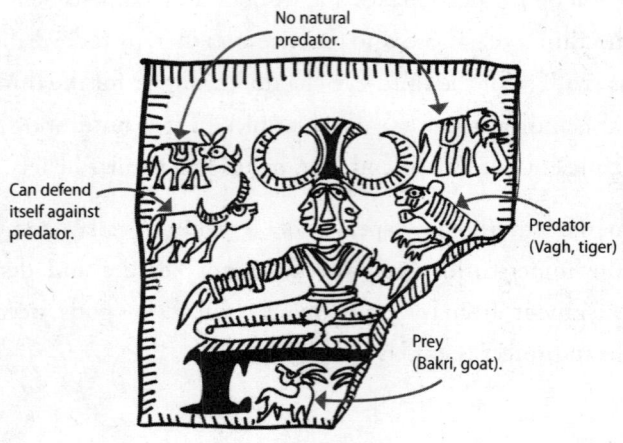

No natural predator.

Can defend itself against predator.

Predator (Vagh, tiger)

Prey (Bakri, goat).

Pashupati seal.

8. Hunger and Fear

All living organisms seek food. Harrapan seals depict images of crocodiles eating fish, a reminder of the law of the jungle. Harappans showed food trays before animals to symbolize the yearning for resources—need, greed, ambition.

No animal wants to become food. Horns are used by animals to fight predators, establish territory and the pecking order. Harappans used horns as symbols of power.

In later Hindu lore, one-horned beings are linked to contentment and caring.

- ▶ Ganesha, linked to contentment, breaks one of his tusks and uses it as a stylus to write a story about the futility of war. He is known as eka-danta (one-tusked).
- ▶ Vishnu, linked to security, takes the form of a one-horned (eka-shringa) fish (matsya) to tow Manu's ship to safety during a storm.
- ▶ Shiva, who overpowers hunger, is called eka-pada (one who balances himself on one leg).

The 'Pashupati' seals shows animals like the rhinoceros and elephant that were believed to have no natural predator. This indicates luck. The same seal also shows the horned sage separating the tiger (predator) form the buffalo (prey) and the goat (prey). In the presence of a sage, the tiger (vagh) does not attack the goat (bakri). This is how Dilmun, the paradise of Sumerian mythology, is also described.

Buffalo sacrifice in post-monsoon rituals.

Sacrificed head. Worshipper. Markhor goat. Deity.

Goat sacrifice in pre-monsoon rituals.

Script showing seeds sprouting. Goat with vegetation-like tail. Crowns with vegetation.

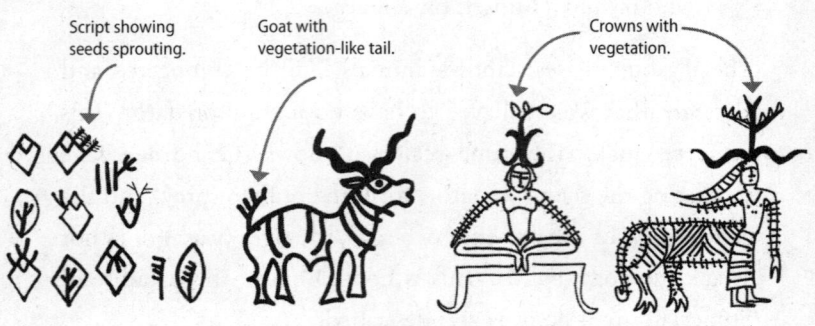

Images suggesting germination, so fertility.

9. Fertility and Sacrifice

Many symbols in the Harappan script show a yearning for blossoming and germination—in other words, a celebration of fertility. The four months of monsoons marked the calving and mating season of wild cattle, buffaloes and bison. It was the time when Palla fish moved upstream through the Indus to spawn. This was the time for summer crops—millets, cotton, rice. Then, after the rains, came the winter harvest of barley and wheat and peas. The nomads came down from the mountains and the goats gave birth in the spring.

So spring (before the monsoon) and autumn (after the monsoon) were times when sacrifices of male goats and male buffaloes were offered to the earth goddess, in exchange for the rich vegetation she gave. This is common in most tribal communities. The earth produces vegetation and in exchange receives blood. Harappan seal art shows the sacrifice of markhor being made to vegetation deities.

Across pastoral and agricultural communities, even today, the female is never sacrificed as she can bear children. Young virgin males are sacrificed to the goddess. Buffaloes and goats and sheep are preferred over bulls as the castrated bull (ox) can be used as a beast of burden. Thus, economics shapes what is sacrificed.

Sumerian art showing a bull (Taurus, Winter) battling a lion (Leo, Summer).

From Sumerian art (2500 BC)

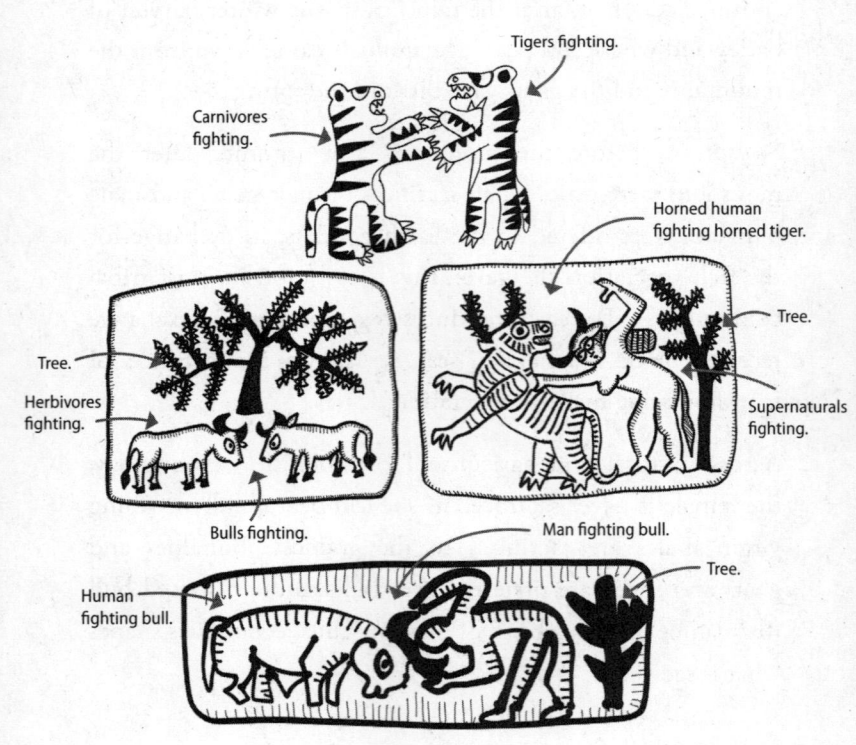

Tigers fighting.

Carnivores fighting.

Horned human fighting horned tiger.

Tree.

Tree.

Herbivores fighting.

Supernaturals fighting.

Bulls fighting.

Man fighting bull.

Tree.

Human fighting bull.

From Harappan seal (2500 BC).

Territorial Beasts.

48   *Ahimsa*

10. Territories and Domination

First came seals with geometric patterns. Then seals with animal figures. Then seals that told stories.

The story seals show domination, animals fighting each other or humans territory:
- ▶ Bulls fighting over territory.
- ▶ Tigers fighting over territory.
- ▶ Horned tigers fighting horned humans.
- ▶ Humans fighting bulls.

All these indicate a clamour over resources: the need to establish a pecking order. Almost all images have a tree in the background—a thorny tree (shami or acacia), indicating the wilderness. In the wild, the strong dominate the weak. It's jungle law. As per the Vedas, such behaviour is 'dharma' of animals, not for humans.

Epics like the Ramayana and Mahabharata are about brothers fighting over property. Vali and Sugriva are monkeys fighting over Kishkinda. The Pandavas and Kauravas are fighting over the kingdom. These are not unique to India. Sumerian art shows bull-like humans fighting tigers. The Old Testament of the Bible informs us the farmer Cain kills the herder Abel.

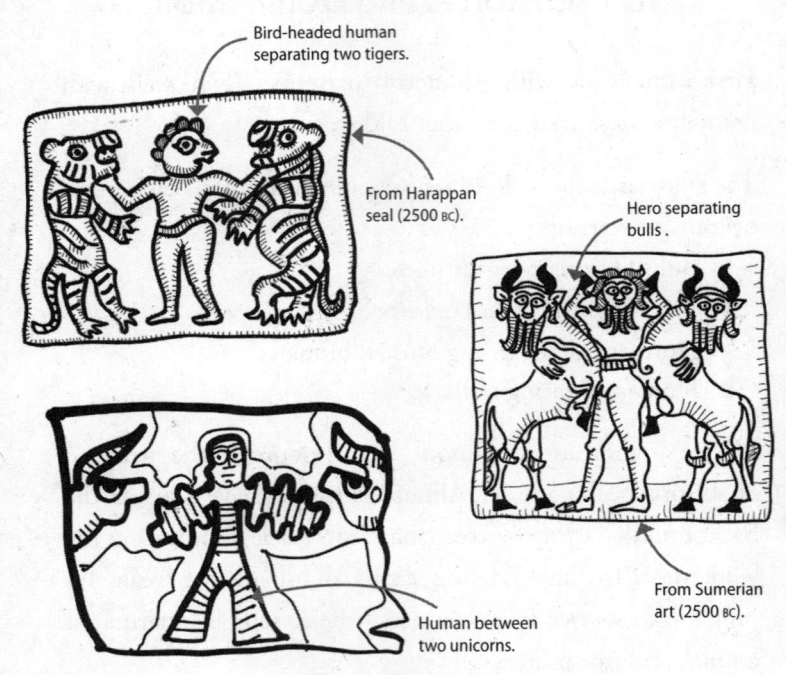

- Bird-headed human separating two tigers.
- From Harappan seal (2500 BC).
- Hero separating bulls.
- Human between two unicorns.
- From Sumerian art (2500 BC).

Separating territorial beasts.

- Hero separating tigers.

Stone Age art from Ratnagiri, western coast of India, showing a man separating two territorial tigers.

11. Beast Master

Since the Stone Age, humans have created artwork that shows man dominating beasts. There are images of humans separating two beasts of the same species that are locked in conflict: tigers, serpents, bulls. This artwork is called 'beast-master'. Pashu-pati, in Sanskrit.

In Harappan seals, there are images showing rivals being separated.
- ▶ A bird-headed being separating two tigers.
- ▶ A man with bangles separating two unicorns.

Such separation of rival beasts by a human is found in Sumer too. Do they indicate that humans are a more dominant species? Or do they show that humans have a different way of life, one where there is no need to dominate or fight? One based on sharing and trading, on exchanging rather than extracting?

We can force animals to submit to our will. But we can hope to reason with humans, even empathize with them. That is the only way to avoid slavery and war.

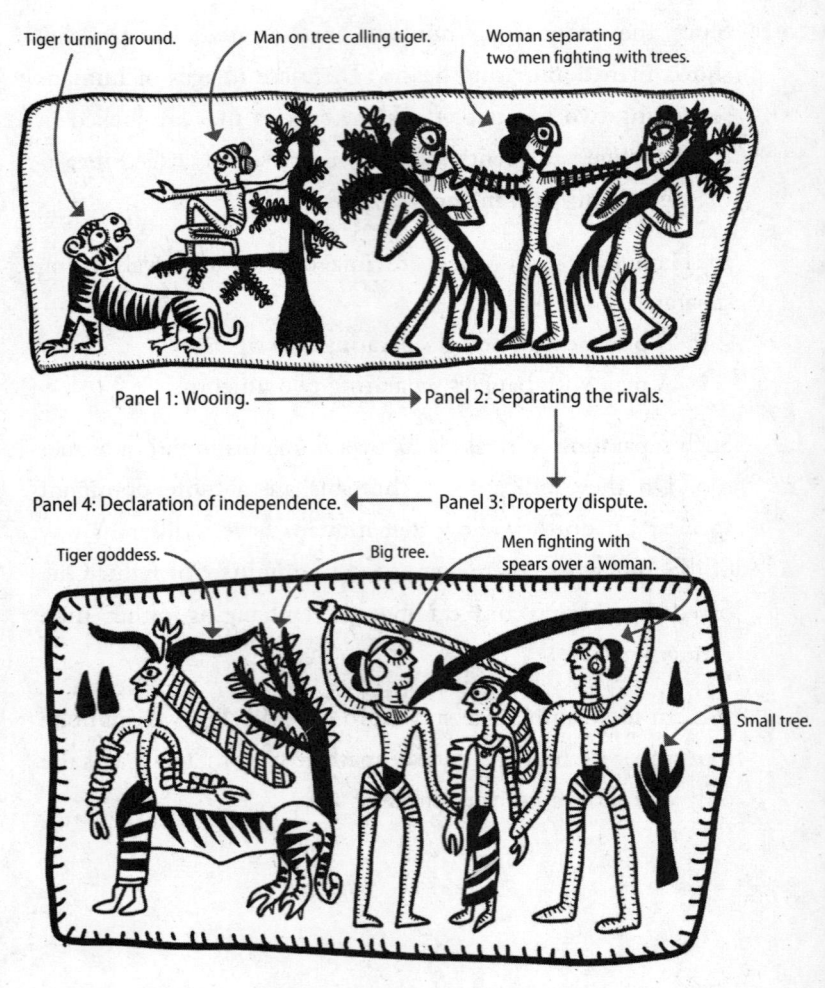

*Woman between two fighting men
(Four panels of one story. World's first comic?).*

12. Tiger Lore

There are two tiny artworks, found in two distant cities of Mohenjo-daro and Kalibangan, where two humans are shown fighting. In each case a woman stands between them. Both seals have tigers too.

- ▶ On a clay tablet a woman separates two men fighting with uprooted trees. Nearby is a thorny tree on which sits a young man wooing a tiger that turns around to look at him.
- ▶ On a cylinder seal, next to a small tree, are two men fighting with spears, each one holding one arm of a woman who stands between them. Further away, next to a taller and thorny tree, is a goddess with a horned crown, whose lower half is that of a tiger.

Neither image celebrates violence. We can join the dots in many ways to compose a story. Here is one based on a popular romantic myth involving shape-shifting nymphs. The nymph breaks the man's heart as she refuses to be controlled by the rules of domestication (monogamy? fidelity?). The man tries to hold on to the nymph by hiding her animal covering, but one day she finds it and escapes in the form of: a seal in Ireland, a swan in Germany, and maybe a tigress in the Indus realm.

Sumerian artworks glorify war. Such artwork is not found in Harappa. When two humans fight there is always a woman between them. Is she trying to make them see reason? Why is it difficult to assume that?

1.

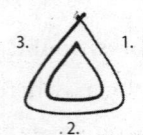

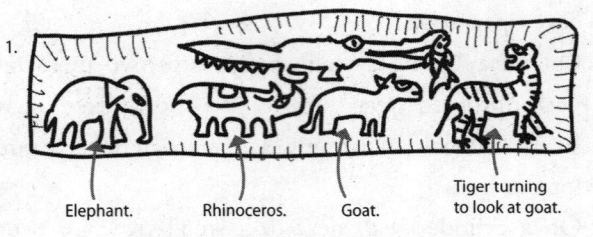

- Elephant.
- Rhinoceros.
- Goat.
- Tiger turning to look at goat.

Wild realm where might is right.

2.

- Unicorn.
- Goat.
- Bison.
- Buffalo.

Domestic pastures.

3.

- Territorial goat.
- Man behind bent woman (sex?).
- Herder.

Human realm of control.

Three-sided clay seal showing a narrative.

54   Ahimsa

13. Forest and Pastures

A tiny clay three-sided tablet, from Mohenjo-daro (M-489), created using temporary wooden moulds, shows three different images:

- One depicts wild animals facing one direction: the elephant, the rhinoceros, a goat, and a tiger turning back. There is also a crocodile eating a fish.
- The other shows a crocodile but without the fish and domesticated animals (goat, bison, buffalo), followed by a unicorn, all facing the same direction.
- The third side shows humans. One separating two goats (though the human can be seen as a tree that is shared by the two goats). One appears sexual (very rare) with a male figure standing behind a bent female. The third seems to be a composite beast, or a herder with a goat.

Seen together they show a wild world, a domesticated world, and the power of humans over nature. In Sumerian myth, nature is chaos and god-like humans bring order. In Indian myth, nature is orderly, where humans play no role. Culture creates the delusion of human control. Sama Veda therefore classifies lyrics of the Rig Veda into two types of melodies:

- Those to be sung in the forest (where humans have no control).
- Those to be sung in the settlement (where humans have control).

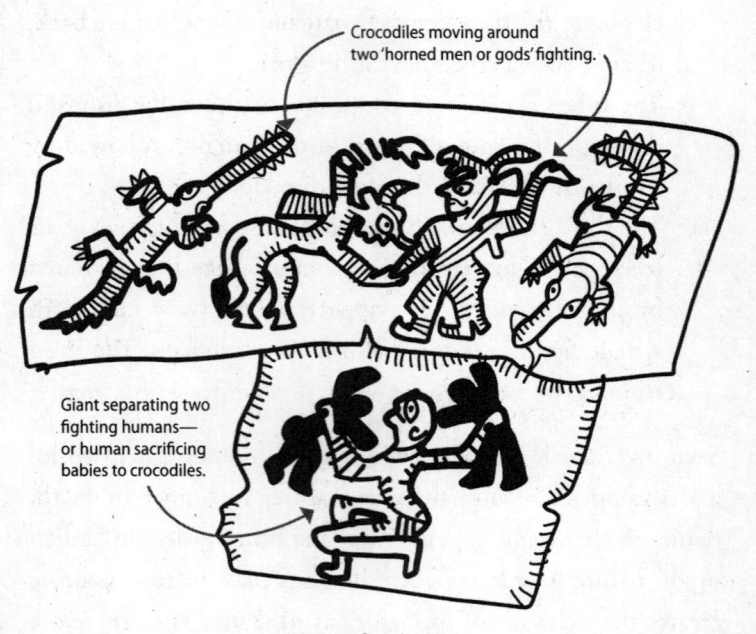

Acts of violence.

14. War and Peace

In Dholavira, there is a tablet with two scenes, one on each side.

- ▶ One side shows only a scene without text: two horned-beings in combat. (Clearly the horned beings are not always non-violent yogis.) Framing this violence are two crocodiles, one on either side, one facing up and the other facing down. This is another depiction of a fight for domination and territory. Is this a fight between two merchant-sailors for control of sea routes?
- ▶ On the other side is a scene with some text. A being holding two humans, one in each hand. Is he a giant god or demon holding two normal-sized humans or a horned priest holding two babies? Or is this just an artistic expression showing a large (wise) woman stopping two small (foolish) men from fighting using either brute force or the force of her argument?

Some see this tablet as indicative of primitive people sacrificing children to crocodiles. Others as a hero myth, like Bhima overpowering the man-eating villain, Bakasura, in an attempt to create an ecosystem of collaboration (dharma) rather than combat and conflict.

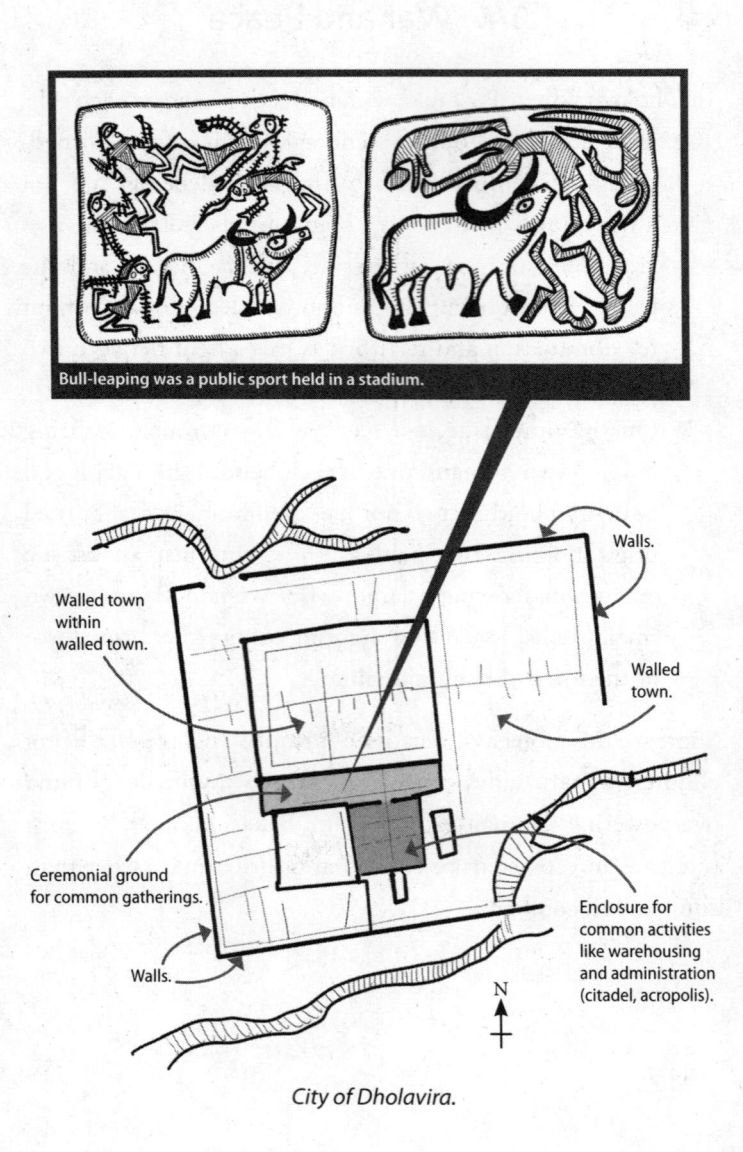

Bull-leaping was a public sport held in a stadium.

- Walls.
- Walled town within walled town.
- Walled town.
- Ceremonial ground for common gatherings.
- Walls.
- Enclosure for common activities like warehousing and administration (citadel, acropolis).

N

City of Dholavira.

Ahimsa

58

15. Who Unites the Divided?

Harappan cities were a set of gated communities each belonging to a clan. They shared a common area. Archaeologists refer to these common areas in different Harappan cities as citadel (European term), acropolis (Greek term) and block (American term). They contained warehouses, secretariats, common bathing areas and gathering halls, but no temples or palaces.

Who got the competitive clans to collaborate? As per the seventeenth-century Hindu text *Keralolpathi,* when Parashurama realized that Brahmin clans in Kerala would never agree on any issue, he ordered them to submit to a foreign ruler, a Chera. This 'stranger king' alone had the power to punish the defiant, but could not benefit from his power. In other words, he had to be a monk—one who renounced all worldly goods, pleasures and relationships. Was this the horned sage?

This idea of using an outsider to govern a local territory was common in early India. Many local warlords and chieftains invited Brahmins or Buddhist or Jain monks to serve as administrators. The hermit-administrator (shramana) was seen as spiritual and therefore fair. People also venerated them as upasaka.

Horned figurine.

Horned mask.

- Flowing hood.
- Bangles.
- Belly (pregnant?).

Horned sage seated on low stool.

Horned sage standing between trees.

16. Horned Sage

Sumerian gods wore horned crowns. Are Harappan seals with horned beings representative of gods? Are the horns emerging from their heads or simply part of a helmet or crown? It is not clear. Sometimes there are horned beings with tails. Are these the same as the sages? Is that an animal skin worn by a human or a fantastic beast—half human, half animal? None of this is clear. Herbivores have horns to protect themselves. Harappan art shows horns of bulls, buffaloes, bison, goats and antelope. Between the horns is a tuft of either feathers or vegetation.

The horned being is shown in many contexts:
- ▶ Seated on a stool.
- ▶ Standing.
- ▶ Standing among trees.
- ▶ Offering obeisance to another horned being.
- ▶ Fighting a horned being.
- ▶ Fighting a horned animal.
- ▶ Guarding cattle.

Buddhist and Hindu lore, composed 1,500 years after the Harappan period, speaks of a horned sage, Rishya-shringa-muni, born when a hermit copulated with a doe. He knew no women, so was celibate. And this gave him magical powers to cause droughts. To bring back rain, women were dispatched to seduce him. Did the Harappans also fear the power of the hermit who gave up all worldly attachments? Did they see him as capable of causing droughts?

Bull-man with bow.

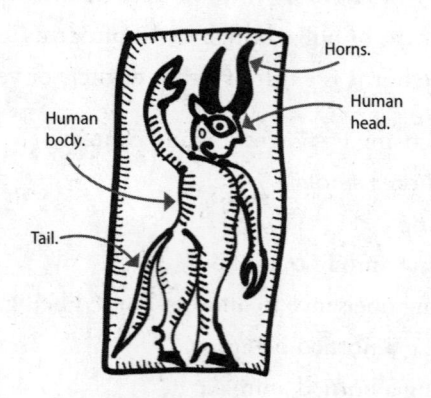

Bull-man waving.

Bull-man with animals.

17. Bull-man

On a tiny copper plate, roughly 2 cm x 4 cm, is an image of a horned man with a bow. While horned men are common in Harappan art, bows are not. The man also has a tail. It is tough to figure out if the man is wearing an animal pelt or is himself a fantastic beast. Is he hunting tigers and leopards who threaten livestock? Another horned man with a tail is shown waving his hand. Yet another is shown raising his hand to a markhor and a unicorn.

In European traditions, horned beings are linked to the Devil. But in Hinduism, horned beings can be good (Nandi, bull of Shiva) or bad (Mahisha, buffalo killed by Durga). There is a tribe in Maharashtra who use bison horns as a sacred headdress. Men and women with horned headdresses seem to evoke awe and respect in Harappan art.

The horned headdress signified some form of power. Maybe not one of brute force, but a moral force born by outgrowing natural human instincts like hunger and fear. One whose aura gets people to work together. A forerunner of later Pashupata kings who ruled South and Southeast Asia after AD 500?

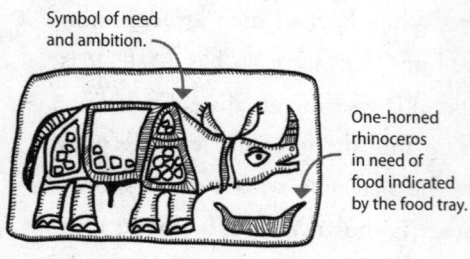

Rhinoceros with tray.

- Symbol of need and ambition.
- One-horned rhinoceros in need of food indicated by the food tray.

Unicorn with an object that may be an incense burner.

- Upturned head, as if sniffing perfume from below or alert to threats in the air from beyond.
- Incense burner.

Unique pendant with unicorn.

- Womb within.
- Womb without.
- Incense burner.

Ahimsa

18. Mythical Unicorn

The Harappan unicorn is found in nearly 80 per cent of the 2,000 stamp seals found, but not on the 'Pashupati' seal. Clay figurines of this one-horned animal suggest that Harppans did imagine a mythical creature, unrelated to any clan, one who craves nothing but benefits all. The ideal 'stranger-king'. Perhaps the unicorn was the symbol of the horned hermits of Harappa who managed inter-clan and inter-city affairs.

Nearly 1,500 years after the Harappan period, India was dominated by merchants who were householders (shravaka) and venerated Buddhist and Jain hermits (shramana). Hermits encouraged traders to shun hoarding, to repay and write off debts and use trade to enable rather than dominate. Thus, concepts of debit (paap), credit (punya) and karma (balance sheet) emerged. Did this have ancient Harappan roots? The householders represented by two-horned animals and hermits by the one-horned unicorn?

The one-horned rhinoceros has needs so is often shown with a food tray. But the unicorn is shown enjoying only perfume from an incense burner. Very few seals show male genitalia. One pendant shows a unicorn with a womb positioned within a womb, as if representing a metaphysical idea: what is within is without.

Unicorn.

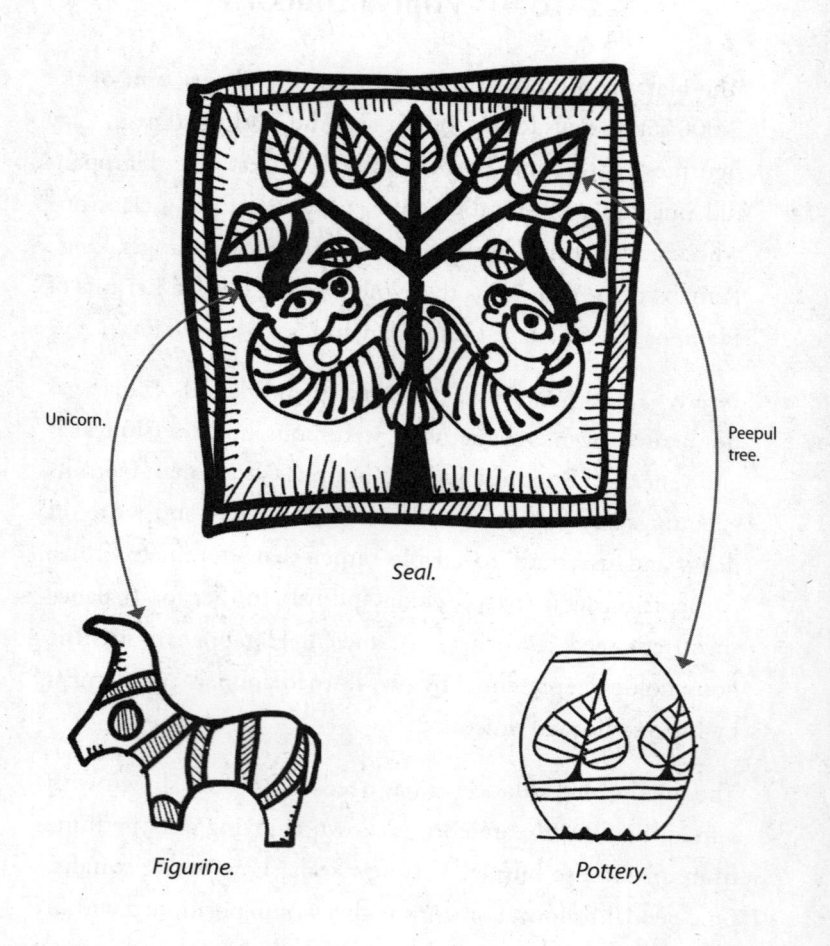

Peepul tree.

Seal.

Figurine.

Pottery.

19. Tree of Mendicants

A distinguishing feature of Harappan pots is the presence of peepul leaves.

Peepul, though revered, is never planted inside the house as it can destroy the walls and foundations. It is said to be the residence of ghosts. So just as Harappans buried the dead outside the city, the venerated peepul would always be on the outskirts of the village, where villagers would go to meet wandering mendicants.

The peepul tree bears flowers before the rains, which turn into fruit during the monsoon. The monsoon season is traditionally when hermits in India stay in one place and avoid wandering, a practice that may have ancient roots.

In one seal, the unicorn is linked to the peepul tree, emerging from it. This reaffirms the connection between the unicorn and hermits. The Buddhists sang a song that a hermit must be like the solitary horn of a one-horned beast. Most people assume the one-horned beast is the rhinoceros. But it could be the unicorn. In Chinese lore, unicorn was a deer-like one-horned beast from a land far away who was used by judges to identify and impale liars. These could be memories of a time when hermits served as arbitrators in trading disputes.

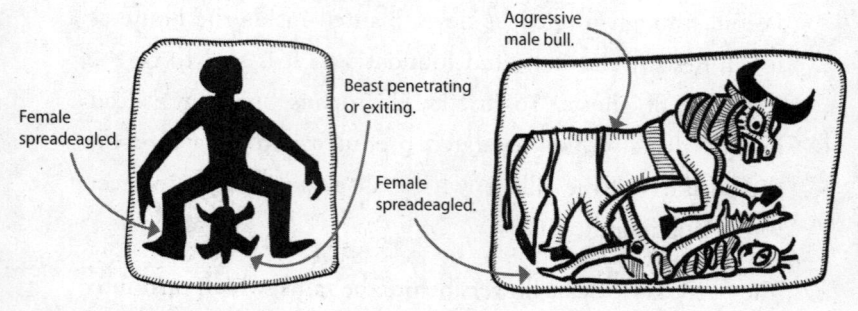

Woman either copulating with, or giving birth to, a crocodile-like creature.
- Female spreadeagled.
- Beast penetrating or exiting.
- Female spreadeagled.

Bull copulating with or attacking woman.
- Aggressive male bull.

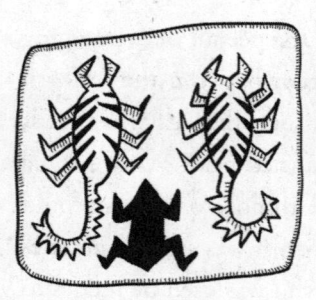

Twin scorpions with frog from Rehman-Dheri.

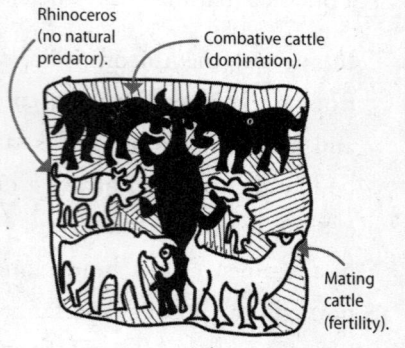

Giant scorpion surrounded by animals.
- Rhinoceros (no natural predator).
- Combative cattle (domination).
- Mating cattle (fertility).

Ahimsa

20. Absence of Romance

There are no romantic images in Harappan seals. Lots of violence, but no love. Even the sexual scenes are rather grotesque—an aroused bull leaping over a spreadeagled woman, a crocodile-like beast either entering a woman's womb or exiting it. There is nothing akin to the Buddhist couple images (mithun) or the Hindu erotic imagery (maithuna). In Sumerian art, though we find images of couples, families and sexual imagery.

The Harappans loved colourful clothes and jewels made of colourful beads. They used shampoo and anointed their bodies with oil and fragrant herbs. They enjoyed games, sport and music. So they loved pleasure. But in romantic and sexual matters, they do not seem to have been very expressive in their art. Was it because of a monastic ideal, where sex was only about reproduction?

Images that signify fertility are few. In an early Harappan seal from Rehman-Dheri we find two scorpions and two goats. Then we find images of scorpions with many animals around them. These suggest fertility and fecundity. But one cannot be sure.

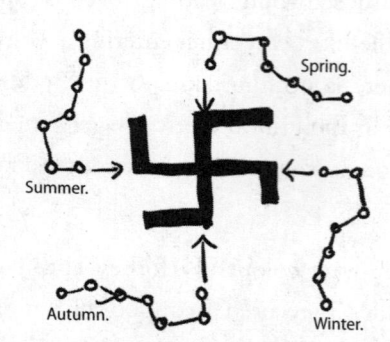

Symbol depicting movement of Big Dipper in northern sky across seasons.

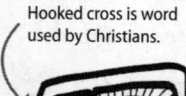

Hooked cross is word used by Christians.

Swastika is word used by Buddhists, Jains, Hindus.

Harappan seal.

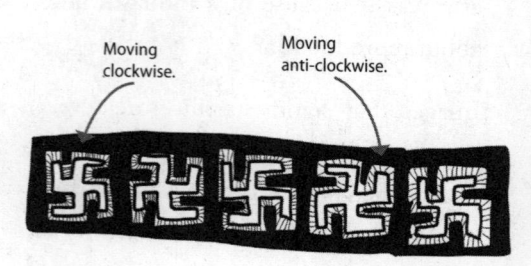

Moving clockwise.

Moving anti-clockwise.

Set of hooked crosses on Harappan clay tablet.

21. Hooked Cross of Happiness

Many cultures around the world, including the Harappans, noticed that the Big Dipper constellation of seven stars (shaped like a giant spoon) rotates in the northern sky. Its orientation marks the different seasons. When its position over spring, summer, autumn and winter is marked, it creates the hooked cross: a symbol of celestial and seasonal rhythms, marking the times to sow seeds, harvest crops, and migrate with animals or anticipate floods or rains.

This hooked cross is known as swastika in Vedic traditions, for the phrase 'su-asti' means to let good things happen. This symbol is found in Harappan seals. This indicates they were aware of the north, and the movement of the Big Dipper over the seasons. In Vedic texts, the Big Dipper is called 'Sapta-Rishi mandala' and is linked to the seven sages.

We do not know if the word 'swastika' or the concept of seven sages existed in Harappan times. But the symbol certainly existed. What it meant then we can only speculate.

Directions were certainly important to Harappans as we see their streets were aligned to the cardinal directions.

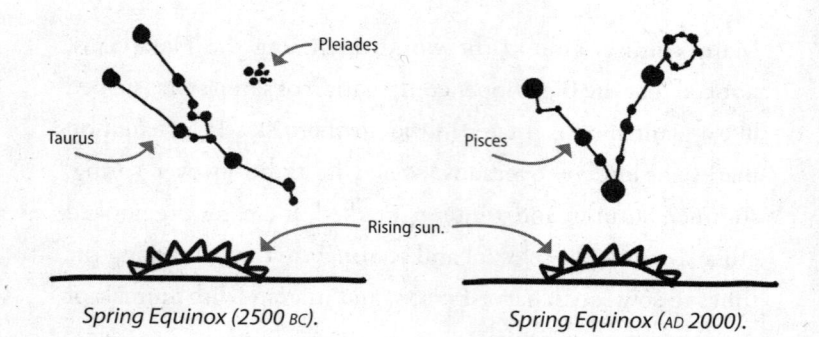

Spring Equinox (2500 BC).

Spring Equinox (AD 2000).

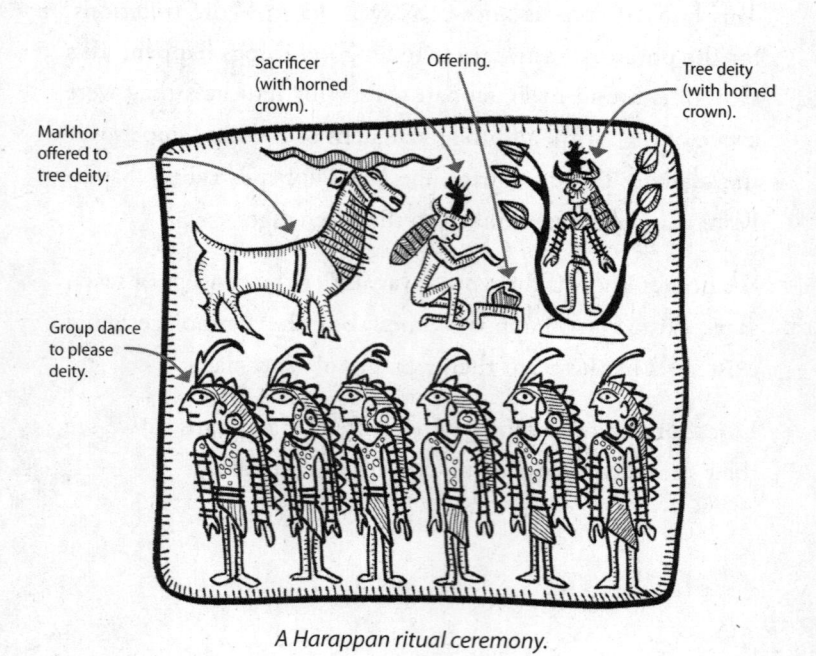

A Harappan ritual ceremony.

22. Seven Sages, Seven Sisters

Tree worship and animal sacrifice is part of many desi (folk) and margi (mainstream) rituals in India. Harappan seals depict this as well. In one famous seal, a markhor is being offered in sacrifice by a devotee wearing a horned helmet to a deity standing between trees—also wearing a horned helmet. There is also an image of seven people dancing. They all have plumage on their heads, a pigtail or hanging hood behind the head, bangles around their arms, and are wearing skirts. Are these seven men or women?

If women, they could represent the seven stars of the Pleiades constellation (Krittika nakshatra) that marked the eastern sky during the Harappan spring. If men, they could be the seven stars of the Big Dipper constellation (Sapta-rishi mandala) that can be seen rotating around the north to this day.

In Vedic literature, the seven sages had seven wives. The sages accused the wives of infidelity and so the wives moved away from the northern sky towards the eastern horizon, to reside with constellation Taurus, the bull (Rishabha rashi). From 4000 to 2000 BC, the sun was in the house of Taurus during the spring equinox, a memory that resurfaces in Shatapatha Brahmana (800 AD). After 2000 BC, it moved towards the house of Aries. Currently it is in the house of Pisces. The shift happens gradually over 2,150 years. Does this Harappan artwork indicate a spring equinox festival?

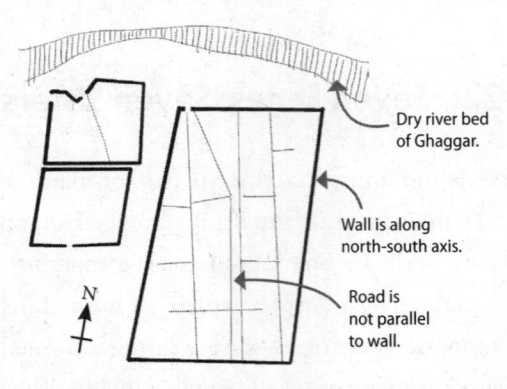

City layout of Kalibangan site in Rajasthan.

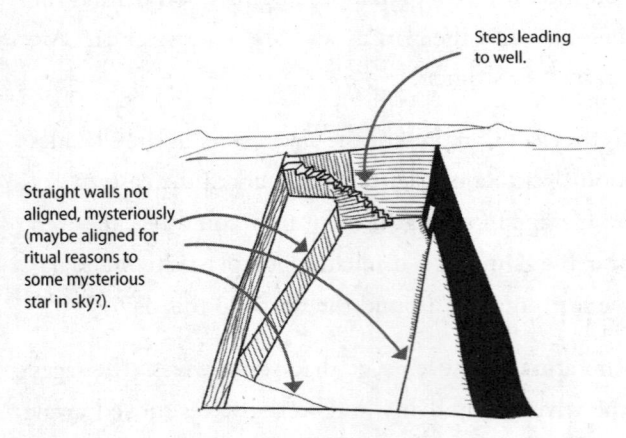

Rock-cut reservoir of Dholavira in Kutch, Gujarat.

Fish with stars from Amri pottery.

Peacock flying towards stars (post Harappan Cemetery H).

23. Starry Sky

The idea of dividing the sky into twenty seven (3x3x3) divisions (nakshatra) is found in the Vedas but not in the Avesta. This was clearly a Harappan memory. The months of the Hindu calendar are named after star clusters near which the full moon occurred when the calendar was being formulated. As per astronomers, the moon was closest to these nakshatra around 3000 BC. This indicates that the Harappans introduced the immigrant Aryans to the nakshatra system of dividing the sky.

Harappans were also drawn to the sky, which is why their cities were laid as a grid, with streets running along the cardinal directions. Alignment with stars seems to be the only explanation for the streets in cities like Kalibangan not being parallel to walls, or for the strange oblique cuts in the rectangular rock-cut wells of Dholavira.

On pottery we do see stars. This includes images of peacocks flying towards the stars, carrying humans in their bellies, and stars in the body of fish. Some scholars argue that the word for star and the word for fish was the same in the Harappan language, as it is in modern Dravidian language—min. So fish symbols in Harappan script refer to stars and constellations.

Venerating a seated sage.
- Half-kneeling stance of devotee or student.
- Meditative pose of sage or master (Bhadra-asana or throne position).

When venerating a tree deity.
- Half-kneeling stance of devotee.
- Standing posture of deity.

Calling out to a tiger.
- Half-kneeling posture.

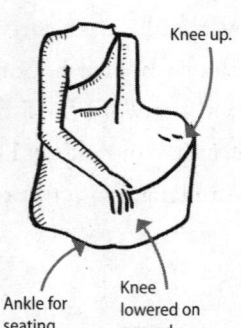

Stance of the statesman or 'priest-king'.
- Knee up.
- Ankle for seating.
- Knee lowered on ground.

24. Harappan Stance

A worshipper is often shown making offerings to a tree or a deity in Harappan art. What is significant is the way the worshipper sits: a half-kneeling position, with one knee on the floor and the other up close to the chest. Many Indians sit this way even today, when working, especially in the kitchen. This stance is also seen repeatedly:

- ▶ When venerating a seated sage.
- ▶ When venerating a tree deity.
- ▶ When calling out to a tiger.
- ▶ Stance of the so called 'priest-king'.

This stance is different from that of the deity who is either standing with his or her legs apart, or seated with soles together on a low stool with arms extended, palms on the knees: a position suggesting meditation.

In Sumerian art, devotees are seen with palms interlocked, gazing upon the deity, either standing or kneeling. Such statues of adoring devotees are not found in Harappan cities.

Some terracotta images, but not seals, show the 'namaste' gesture. Sumerians also kept hands interlocked but not in the namaste (palms together) pose.

Harappan procession.

25. Procession

There is one rare clay tablet that depicts a procession. The images being carried are:
1. A standard that is often seen in front of unicorns on seals.
2. A unicorn or a bull.
3. A flag.
4. A globular object (unclear).

This indicates that there were processions held in the Harappan cities. Such public events are designed to unite people ritually. The tablet suggests that the city authorities wanted to communicate ceremonially. This seems to depict a religious or secular procession held on special days to unite a people or a community. Was this held for one gated community or for the whole city, or for all cities on the same day, at the same time? We have no answers.

In Dholavira, located on an arid island in Kutch, archaeologists have identified a public space with seating arrangements that is called a 'stadium', built by demolishing older residential structures. This may have been used for such processions and for games, like bull-leaping, at the time of market gatherings when sailors would have arrived from Magan (Oman) for the annual trade fair. The north-south streets of all Harappan cities lend themselves to such processions too.

Mighty bull with no food tray, symbol of autonomy.

Man venerating a tree deity.

Village shrine.

- Peepul (sacred fig).
- Cotton threads tied to tree.
- Bull worship (Basava).
- Deepak (oil lamp).
- Nandi (bull of Shiva).
- Rangoli (sacred pattern).
- Purna-kumbha (pot of plenty).

80   *Ahimsa*

26. Temporary Shrines

For over five centuries, nearly twenty generations, the Harappan cities thrived on the banks of the Sindhu and the Saraswati, without temples. The ships sailed up and down rivers and sea-coasts carrying carefully crafted beads, bangles, cloth and furniture, indulging the cravings of Sumerian gods. These five centuries saw the rise of well-planned cities with walls, gates, courtyards, platforms and the seals. There were special pots for rituals too—perforated pots, dishes on stands, images of tiger-women, bull-women and unicorns. Everything disappeared when trade ended.

What continued, and continues till date, amongst farmers, fisherfolk and herdsmen, is the worship of trees and animals, the use of abstract symbols as talismans to evade malevolent forces and attract benevolent ones. Lamps with mustard oil are still used in rituals to ward off ghosts, ghee is used to please deities. White sesame is used for gods of spring, black sesame for ancestors who come in the autumn.

Gods and goddesses who reside in mountains, caves, lakes and trees are invoked through pots filled with leaves and fruits (purna-kumbha), and geometric patterns made using turmeric, cinnabar, grain flour and flowers (rangoli/kolam/muggu). There is no trace left after the ritual. No archaeologist ever finds any evidence of it. No historian knows of it.

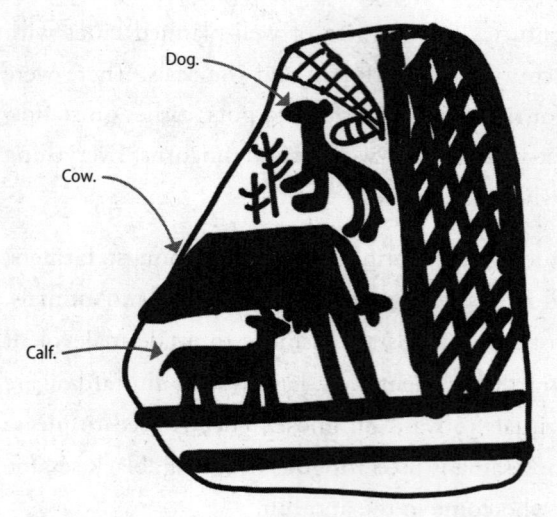

Rare image of cow found in Harappan pottery.

Resources

The oldest Tamil poetry, known as Sangam literature, which is over 2,000 years old, refers to five major landscapes: mountains (kurinji), forests (mulai), fields (marutham), coasts (neithal) and deserts (palai). There are no deserts in Tamil Nadu, but all five landscapes shaped the Harappan civilization. Fields thrived on the banks of two rivers; one has since dried up, though its memory resurfaces in later Vedic literature. Here the humped 'zebu' bull and water buffalo were domesticated. Cows, venerated in later Hinduism, are rare in art, but compensated by the presence of bulls on seals. Farmers traded grain for metal and stone from mountains and deserts. Wood from Himalayan forests was used to build houses. River reeds were used to make boats to sail along coasts to Mesopotamia.

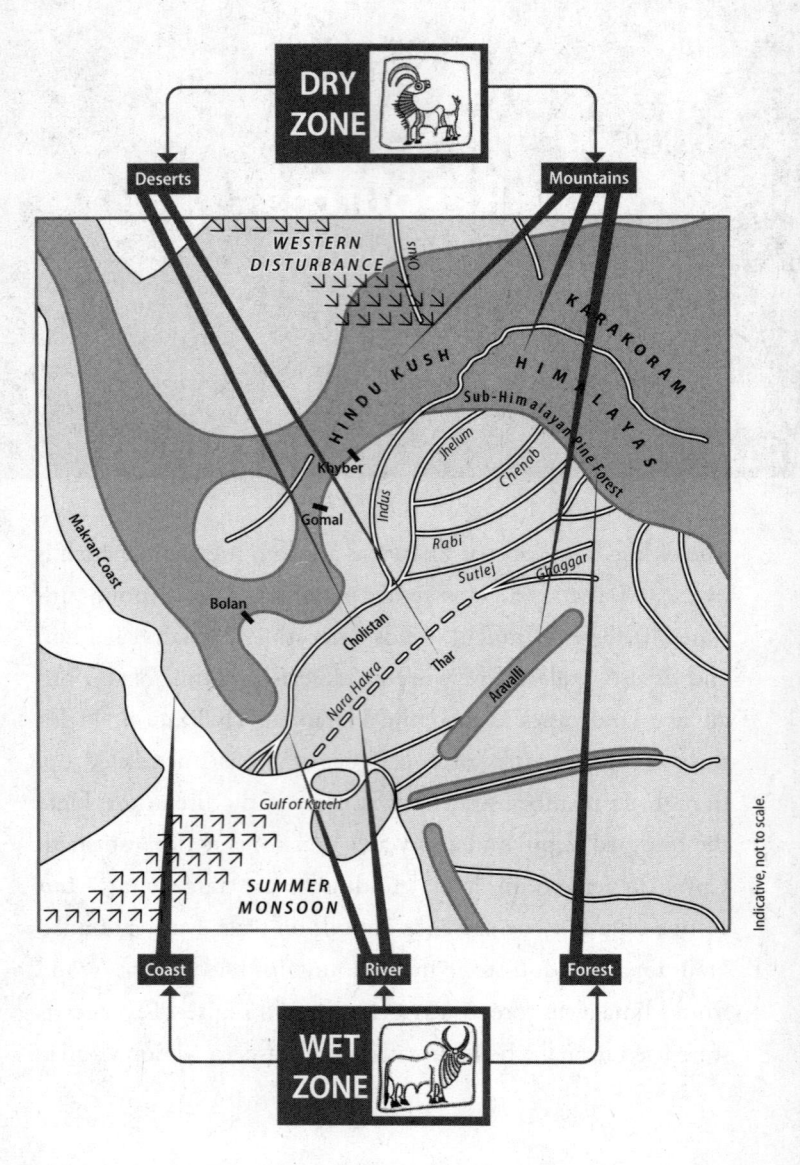

Wet and Dry Zones of Harappan civilization.

27. Two Ecological Zones

The Harappan civilization emerged due to trade between two ecological zones in the Greater Indus Region.

▶ The Wet Zone: The fertile alluvial river systems of Sindhu (Indus) and Saraswati (Ghaggar Hakra), stretching from the sub-Himalayan pine forests in the north to the delta in the south. The southern section received rainfall from the summer monsoon winds, while the northern part got rain in winter due to westerly disturbances. Here agriculture thrived, but there was no mineral wealth. The wet zone includes the long coastline from Gujarat to Makran, which traded with Oman.

▶ The Dry Zone: The mountains (Hindu Kush, Himalayas, Aravalli) and deserts (Kharan, Cholistan, Thar), rich in minerals and stones, but poor agriculture. These were connected via Bolan and Khyber passes to Afghanistan, Central Asia and Iran.

The two zones were connected by nomads who brought wheat and barley to the Indus from Mesopotamia. Maybe, in art, goats symbolize the dry zone, while buffaloes and cattle symbolize the wet zone.

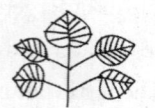

Peepul tree bears fruit.

Water buffaloes give birth and mate.

Palla fish move upstream.

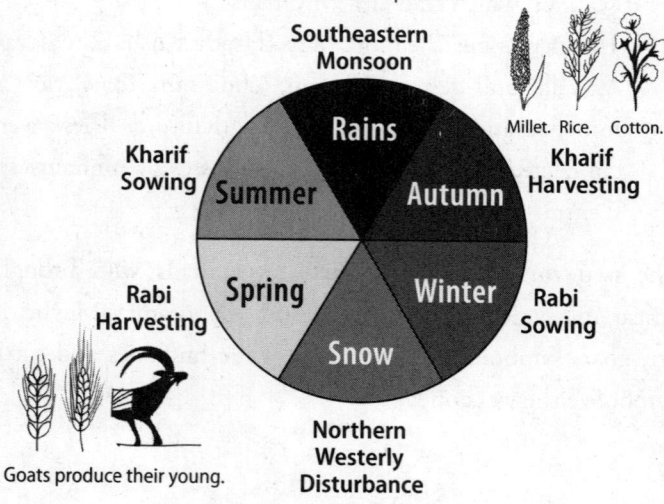

Southeastern Monsoon

Kharif Sowing

Summer — Rains

Autumn — **Kharif Harvesting**

Millet. Rice. Cotton.

Rabi Harvesting

Spring — Winter — **Rabi Sowing**

Snow

Northern Westerly Disturbance

Goats produce their young.

Seasons in the Greater Indus Region.
The seasonal pattern continues to this day.

Ahimsa

28. Seasons

The Greater Harappan Region had six seasons: spring, summer, monsoons, autumn, winter and snow.

The presence of summer monsoon in the south and winter snow in the north made the Indus region more fertile and very different from Mesopotamia and Egypt, which hardly ever experienced rains. This explains why the Harappan civilization was ten times the size of Mesopotamia, and why it was overcrowded as India is even today.

- ▶ During summer, the melting ice and the monsoons from the south caused rivers to flood. This was the time of the summer crops and breeding season for wild cattle. So the wild cattle came to symbolize the monsoon, as did the peepul and acacia trees, whose flowering indicated the onset of the monsoon.
- ▶ In winter, the westerlies from the Mediterranean caused rain and snow on the mountains, forcing nomads to move down towards the plains, in time for the goats to give birth in spring. The symbol for winter and spring was the goat.

The seasons determined the agricultural patterns in the wet zone, the nomadic movements in the dry zone and the trade patterns along the coast. On pots, images of peepul leaves, bulls and goats may not have been decorative. They may have indicated an intimate understanding of seasons.

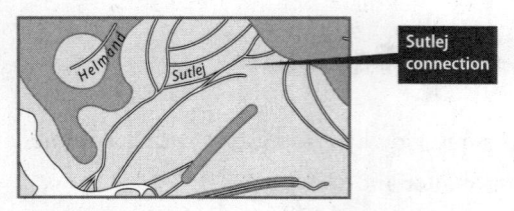

20,000 BC Perennial Saraswati.

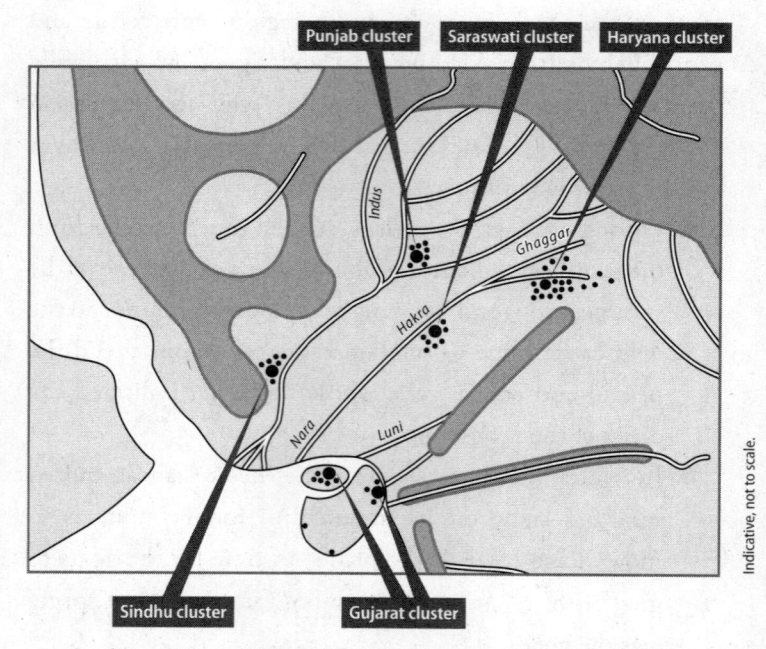

Settlement clusters beyond Indus rivers 4,500 years ago (2500 BC).

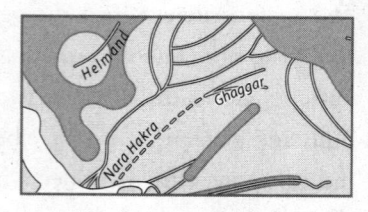

2000 BC Disappearing Saraswati.

29. Parallel River Systems

A century ago, ancient settlements were found in the Indus river basin. Hence, the name 'Indus Valley civilization'.

However, over the past fifty years, many new settlements have been discovered, including the large site of Ganweriwala, clustering in a stretch in the desert of Cholistan, extending to the plain between Sutlej and Yamuna, in present-day Haryana. This indicates the Harappan civilization developed along another river that once flowed east of the Indus.

This invisible river has a very interesting history:
- The river channel was snow-fed until 20,000 years ago, when it was connected to the Sutlej. This was long before any human settlement.
- Then it became rain-fed. Humans settled on its banks 5,000 years ago, using clever water management strategies for the dry seasons. Erratic rain patterns 4,000 years ago forced people to move out. This may have contributed to the fall of the Harappan civilization.
- Currently it has three parts:
  - Ghaggar, where water flows during monsoons, in Himachal and Haryana.
  - Hakra, where water disappears in the Cholistan deserts of Pakistan.
  - Nara, a rivulet that reappears near the Indus delta.

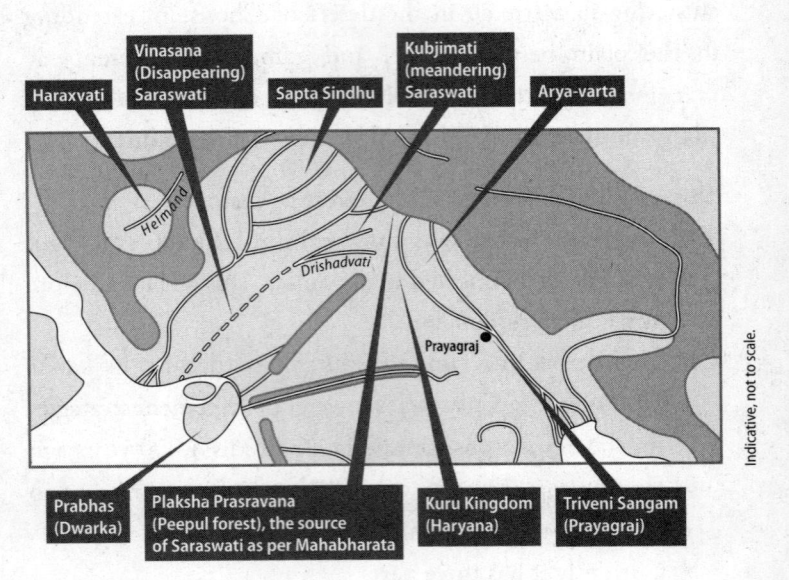

Traditional views on Saraswati river.

30. Saraswati

Many Indians identify the Ghaggar-Hakra river with the Saraswati, mentioned over fifty times in the Rig Veda, which is said to have disappeared in the desert as per later Vedic texts. It is argued that this proves Vedic people lived in Indus cities.

- ▶ The Mahabharata (written around 100 BC) refers to Balarama travelling upstream along the Saraswati from Gujarat to the Himalayas.
- ▶ Even today, people believe the Saraswati flows underground and joins Ganga and Yamuna at Triveni-Prayag-Sangam. This is the explanation given for the vast number of ground water wells in Rajasthan, making Thar one of the most densely populated deserts in the world.

But the chronology is rather messy. Harappan urban settlements thrived before 2000 BC, while the Vedic verses were composed only after 1000 BC. The oldest layers of the Persian Avesta, also composed around 1500 BC, in Iran, refer to the rivers Haraxvati and Hindu. Avesta is clearly talking about Saraswati and Sindhu, since the Indian 's' sound becomes 'h' in Persia. No one doubts that Hindu/Sindhu refers to Indus. But what about Haraxvati/Saraswati?

- ▶ Is it a river in Helmand basin of Afghanistan, that the Aryans crossed as they moved from Central Asia to India?
- ▶ Is it memory of the Ghaggar-Hakra transmitted by post Harappan women who married Aryan migrants?

Bahrain and Oman

Persian Gulf

Baharin

Suktagen-dor

Oman

Dholavira

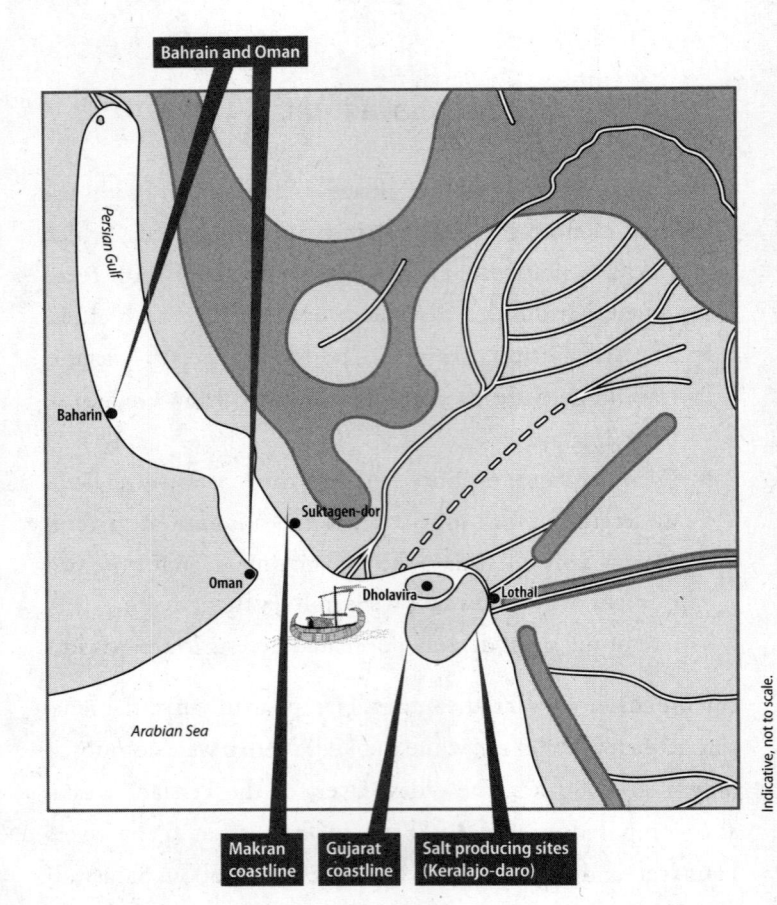

Lothal

Arabian Sea

Indicative, not to scale.

Makran coastline | **Gujarat coastline** | **Salt producing sites (Keralajo-daro)**

Shell collection and salt producing sites.

92   *Ahimsa*

31. Coastline

Around 2300 BC, the world's first empire was established in present-day southern Iraq and Iran by Sargon of Akkad. He boasted that in his docks were ships from Meluhha, the black land, perhaps referring to the brown-skinned people of the coastline around the Indus delta. This explains many Harappan settlements along the coast.

- ▶ Sutkagan-dor is the westernmost coastal settlement from where Oman is about a two-day boat ride. The sailors took advantage of the calm sea and probably even monsoon trade winds.
- ▶ Dholavira stood on an island in Kutch. Currently it is surrounded by sands of salt. But during the monsoon, we can still see the sea around it.
- ▶ Lothal was another coastal Harappan city. It was most probably linked by a northerly shallow sea route to Dholavira. It is famous for water harvesting and water management structures.

Over time, the sea receded and land rose, and Lothal went further inland. Much of coastal Gujarat was submerged following floods and coastal erosion. Did this inspire the Mahabharata tale of how the sea claimed Dwarka, city of the Yadavas? These coastal cities were known for trade in conch-shell bangles and utensils. In later Jain lore (AD 1000), the conch-shell becomes the symbol of Nemi, cousin of Krishna, who lived on the coast in Prabhas, near Girnar.

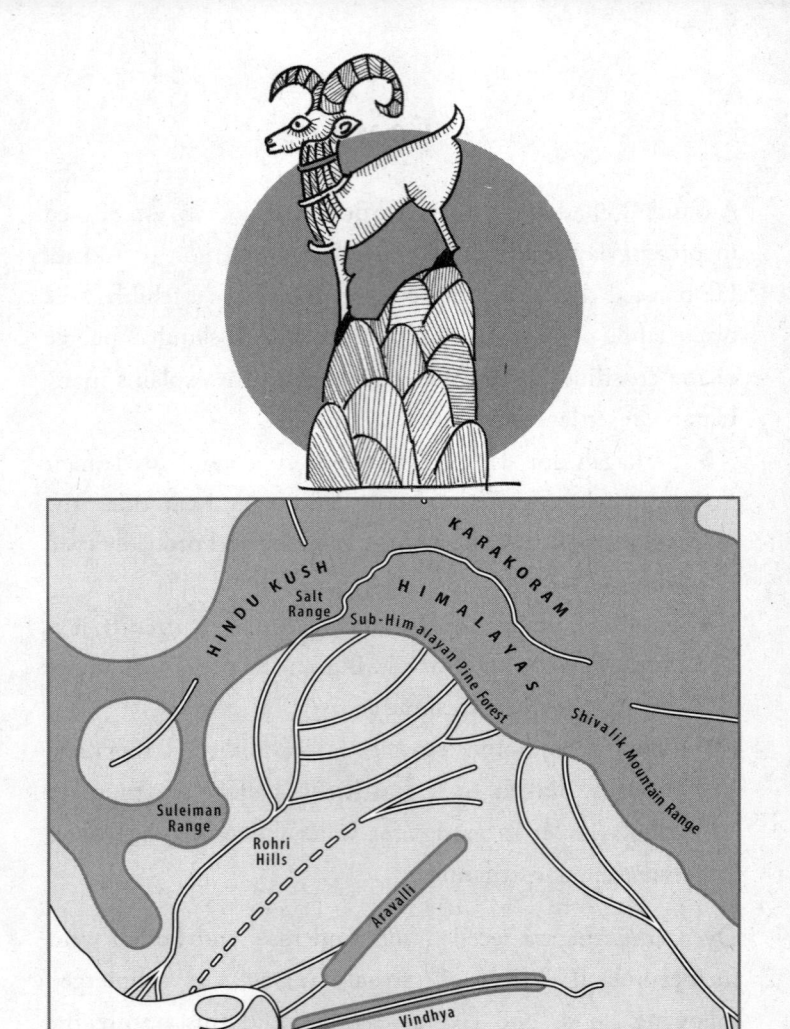

Harappan cities were surrounded by mountains.

32. Mountains

The Greater Indus Region is roofed by mountains: the Hindu Kush in the west, the Himalayas in the north and the Aravalli in the east. There are a few Harappan settlements here indicating their strategic importance. These mountains supplied important raw materials, such as stone, metal and timber from its foothills, to the Indus settlements.

- ▶ Shortugai is located close to the Oxus river and so is a Central Asia outpost of the Harappan civilization that ensured the supply of lapis lazuli and tin through the Gomal Pass, where emerged the site of Rehman-Dheri.
- ▶ Sites in the Iranian plateau, famous for turquoise, were probably accessed through the Bolan Pass, where emerged the site of Mehrgarh.
- ▶ Madan in Akhnoor, Kashmir, is the northernmost settlement, on the banks of the Chenab river, which probably was the source of deodar timber from the Himalayan forests. These would be cut and floated downstream to be picked up by elephants. This wood made its way to faraway Sumer that had no forests.
- ▶ Sites such as Rakhigarhi allowed access to resources in the Aravalli hills, such as copper and hard granite stones.

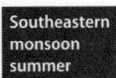

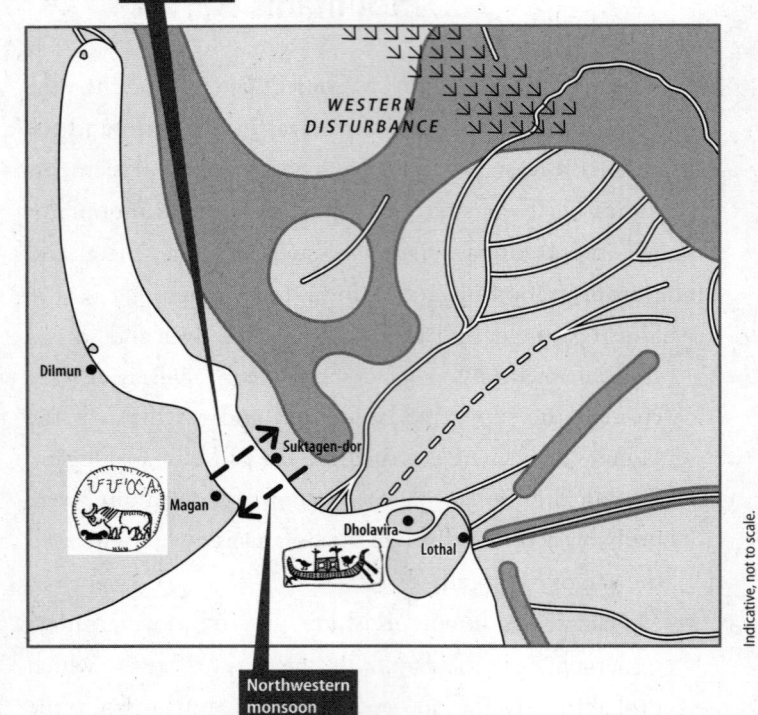

Maritime Harappan trade winds.

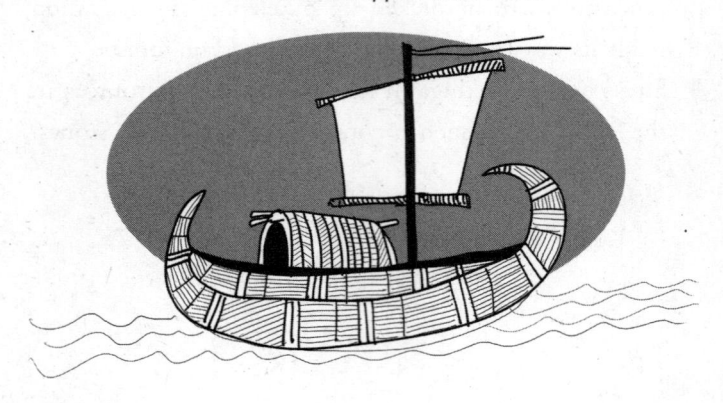

96   Ahimsa

33. Winds

In winter, the northern part of the Greater Indus Region received snowfall. This was because of the Western Disturbance. In summer, the southern part of the Greater Indus Region received monsoon rain.

- ▶ Rain-bearing monsoon clouds would come as the wind blew over the sea from the southwest to the northeast.
- ▶ After the rains ended, in autumn, the wind reversed direction and moved from the northeast to the southwest.

As per Greek writers, this wind pattern was discovered about 2,000 years ago, and exploited for trade. This led to the boom in Indian luxury goods reaching Rome.

However, it seems the monsoon wind patterns were recognized and probably even exploited by the Harappans, over 4,000 years ago, to travel from Meluhha (present-day Makran coast) to Magan (present-day Oman). This is what enabled trade to Dilmun (present-day Bahrain) and Sumer (present-day southern Iraq).

The Harappan seals found in the Gulf region typically have the image of the Indian bison (gaur). This beast is shown docile, with head bent, eating from a tray. This animal is not found in the Gulf, and it breeds in the monsoon season. Could this be symbolic of the merchant guild that had harnessed the power of the monsoons?

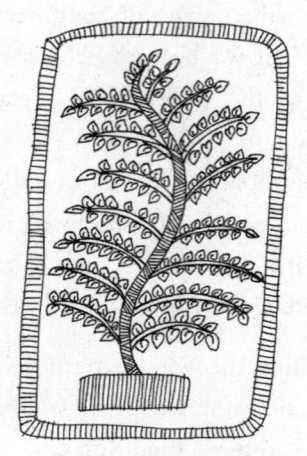

Seal showing a tree.

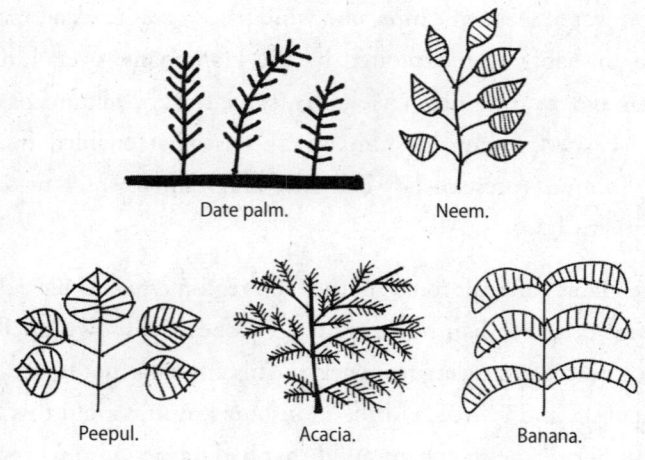

Date palm.   Neem.

Peepul.   Acacia.   Banana.

Common plants shown on pots.

34. Plant Kingdom

Art found on pottery and seals reveals the flora of the forest and fields in the Greater Indus region.

▶ There is a pine wood forest in the sub-Himalayan region. This provided deodar and sheesham (rosewood) timber for housing. Water-resistant teak grows in the southern Gujarat region. This provided timber for building ships that sailed the rivers and even the coasts.

▶ A few plants that are repeatedly represented are those of economic value, which continue to be venerated in India even today. These are: peepul, neem, palm, banana, acacia (babool, khadir) and shami (khejari).

▶ The northern, Sindh, Punjab and Haryana parts of the Indus region are perfect for winter crops: wheat, barley, lentil, peas, mustard and flax. The southern, Gujarat side is perfect for summer crops: millets (ragi, bajra, jowar), rice, sesame and cotton.

▶ Flax was grown in the cooler north for linseed soil and linen. Cotton was grown in the warmer south for cottonseed oil and fabric. Jute was grown in the Indus delta.

▶ Bamboo from Makran and baru grass in Gujarat were used for making reed mats and boats. Tamarisk (jhau) was widely available for fuel. Fruit trees like jujube (ber) and mango grew on the alluvial plains.

Markhor.  Ibex.  Elephant.  Hare.

Animals that appear on seals.

Goat. Humped bull. Deer.

Peacock. Fish. Water buffalo.

Animals that appear on pottery.

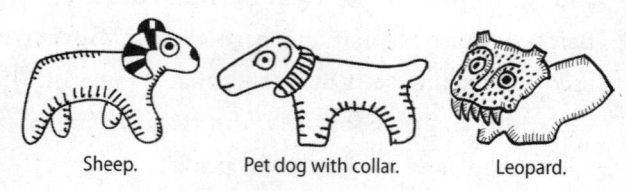

Sheep. Pet dog with collar. Leopard.

Animals that appear as figurines.

35. Animal Kingdom

Harappan art also reveals the fauna, both wild and domestic, found in the Greater Indus region and admired by the Harappans.

- ▶ There were tigers that preyed upon various kinds of deer. It was a region where the rhinoceros roamed with the elephant, which may or may not have been domesticated.
- ▶ The sheep and goat were first domesticated in Mesopotamia. Domesticated goats appear to be preferred over sheep as they are not fussy eaters and could also be used to transport goods up to 20 per cent of their body weight. The region had its share of wild goats: long-horned ibex and the screw-horned markhor.
- ▶ Water buffaloes and humped cattle were domesticated in India. The wild Indian bison (gaur) was a popular symbol.
- ▶ The Harappans had pet dogs with collars, and cats, but they did not worship them as the ancient Egyptians did. Dogs were clearly more popular than cats, maybe because they were used to herd sheep.
- ▶ The chicken was domesticated in the Indus region. Birds that the Harappans were familiar with include peacocks, partridges, parrots and pigeons.
- ▶ Freshwater and saltwater fish were part of the Harappan diet. Especially popular was the bony palla fish that lived in the estuary but swam up the river Indus to breed, like the salmon.
- ▶ Conch shells, which are obtained from conches—a type of marine snail—are found along the Gujarat and Makran coastlines.

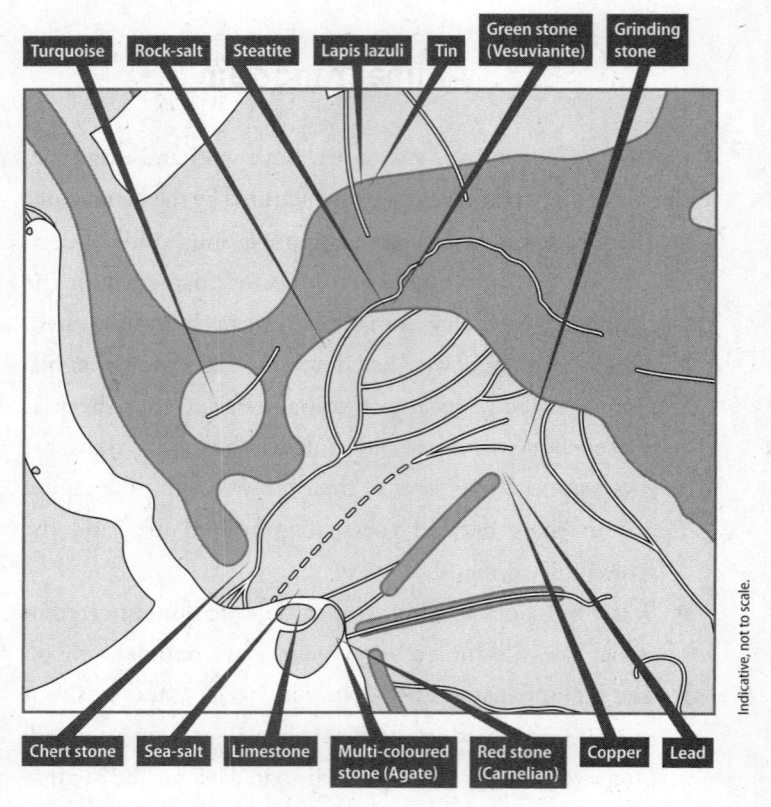

Circle of minerals.

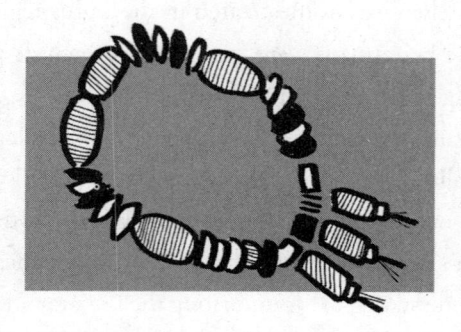

Beaded necklace of semi-precious stones and metal beads.

36. Mineral Kingdom

The Harappan cities were located in the wet zones watered by rivers. This was circled by a dry zone that provided salt, metal and stones.

- ▶ Salt came from the mountains (salt range) and from the sea.
- ▶ Hard stones for griding came from the Suleiman hills, Himalayan foothills and the Aravalli (Kaliana). Limestone came from Dholavira in the south. Chert stones, used for making sharp knives, were found in the Rohri hills of Sindh.
- ▶ The soft stone steatite, which turned white when heated, came from Hazara in Kashmir. Black steatite came from Khyber.
- ▶ Coloured stones for beads came from many locations:
  - Vesuvianite (green) from Baluchistan and Khyber.
  - Lapis lazuli (blue) from Afghanistan.
  - Turquoise (blue) from Iran.
- ▶ Agate (multi-coloured) and Carnelian (red) from Gujarat.
  - Tin came from far away Afghanistan. Gold came from either the Himalayan rivers or was imported, like silver.
- ▶ Copper came from the Aravalli.

Like Harappan cities, Mesopotamian cities were located in the wet zone and traded with the dry zone. But unlike Harappan cities, the Mesopotamian cities fought each other and even fought mountain raiders. Wet and dry zones were in constant conflict in the Middle East, but Harappans found a way to co-exist.

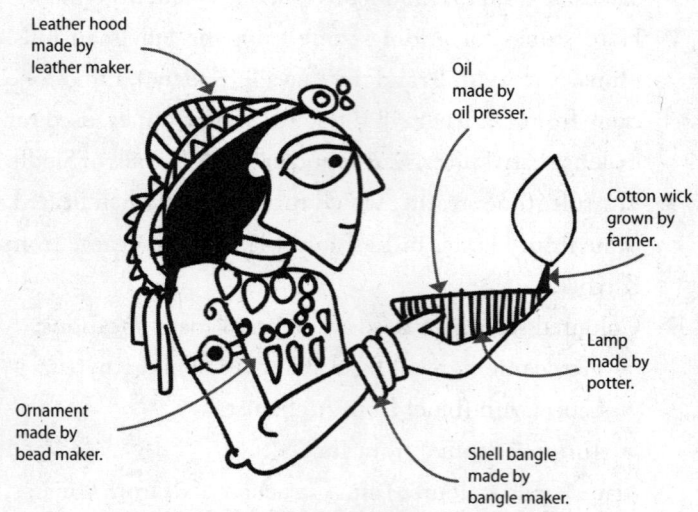

Harappan woman holding oil lamp.

Ahimsa

Knowledge

The presence of tools indicates the presence of humans—and the more refined the tool, the more refined their knowledge. Since Harappan times, knowledge has been transmitted over generations, improved over time, jealously guarded by families, and very occasionally transmitted, giving rise to tribes, clans and castes (jati). Much later, in Sanskrit language, knowledge came to be known as 'mantra', skills as 'tantra', and tools as 'yantra'. Every 'jati' had all three. In the Vedas , service-providers would be categorized as 'shudra', the legs of the organism whose trunk is constituted by merchants (vaishya), arms by warriors (kshatriya) and head by shamans, priests or prophets (brahmana). Merchants, warriors and priests came and went, but the service-providers remained, serving as the foundation of Indian civilization.

Harappans introduced the world to brightly dyed cotton fabric.

106   *Ahimsa*

37. Inventions and discoveries

The Harappan civilization is known for many discoveries and inventions:

- Cotton fabrics.
- Wild silk thread used for stringing beads.
- Sesame oil.
- Needle eye for stitching.
- Moulds for making bricks.
- Urban plan with grid-layout.
- Rain-water harvesting technology.
- Step wells.
- Public baths.
- Indoor baths and latrines.
- Centralized drainage.
- Public garbage bins.
- Dockyards.
- Stadiums.
- Sourcing lapis lazuli and tin, from Afghanistan and beyond.
- Touchstone for identifying gold.
- Lost wax technique for making bronze statues.
- Circular bronze saw.
- Bow drill for making holes in beads.
- Beer strainers.
- Masala.
- Shampoo.
- Ivory tools and miniature pots for cosmetics.
- Etching of carnelian beads.
- Cockfighting.
- Dice.
- A seven-stone game.
- Soak pits for toilets.
- Storm drains for streets.
- Public garbage 'bins'.

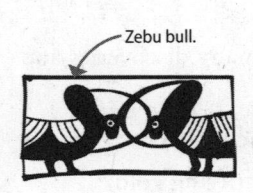

Zebu bull.

Water buffalo.

Pig (rare pottery from Rehman-Dehri).

Animals domesticated in Indus region.

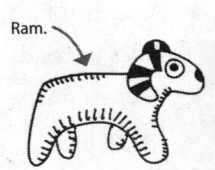

Ram.

Goat.

Domesticated animals imported from Mesopotamia.

Harappans were lactose intolerant (unlike Aryans) and so curdled milk.

Milk came from cows, buffaloes and maybe goats.

Harappan woman churning butter.

Ahimsa

38. Herding

Hunters became herders. In the Indus river valleys the water buffalo and the humped cattle (zebu) were domesticated.

Pigs were also domesticated locally, and used to clean sewage. They were consumed too. Wild asses found in the Kutch region were never tamed. Domesticated goats and sheep were introduced to the Indus region by nomads who came via the Bolan Pass to the Kacchi plains.

Most animals were bred for meat, hide, bones and horn. Cattle dung was used as fuel and as plaster for floors and walls of houses. Castrated bulls (oxen) were used as beasts of burden to pull carts over unpaved dirt roads. Sheep were bred for wool. Goats were also used to transport salt, metal and small stones form the mountains.

The Harappans also established dairies. Like most people in the world (other than those who had the Aryan gene), the Harappans were lactose intolerant, so the milk was turned into curds for consumption. They probably invented the process of turning butter into ghee, which continues to be an Indian staple.

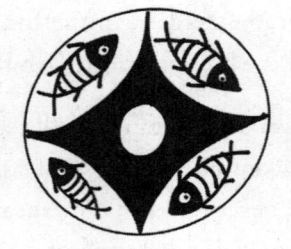

Fish hooks.

Fish art found on pottery.

Pottery showing fisherfolk with nets.

Fishing.

Harappan holding palla fish.

Ahimsa

39. Fishing

Harappans ate fish. Fish came from rivers, ponds and the sea. Saltwater fish were not only caught but also dried and salted and transported to cities further inland.

Copper hooks have been found—some very long ones—suggesting fishing in open seas, far from the coast. Images depict the use of nets and baskets to catch fish. There are terracotta balls that were used to line and weigh down the fishing nets.

The palla (bony) fish moves upstream in the monsoon season and remains a delicacy in the Sindh region. It became the symbol of holy men (pir) in later times, symbolizing those who travel against the current. Fish, and fish scales, are a common motif in Harappan pottery. In art, there are images of crocodiles eating fish, a symbol of the threats faced by fisherfolk, and the law of the jungle that the big eat the small.

Like herders, farming life was resilient against the rise and fall of cities. Like herders, farmers also did not live within Harappan cities. They would have taken their produce into the urban areas through the many gates, as vendors still do today in India.

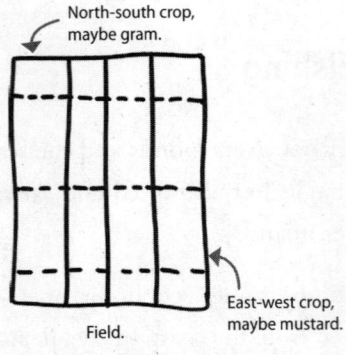

Ploughed field from Kalibangan.
- North-south crop, maybe gram.
- East-west crop, maybe mustard.
- Field.

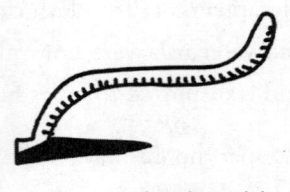

Terracotta plough model found in Banawali.

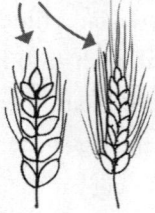

Winter crops.
- Wheat.
- Barley.
- First domesticated in Mesopotamia (grown in Punjab, Haryana).

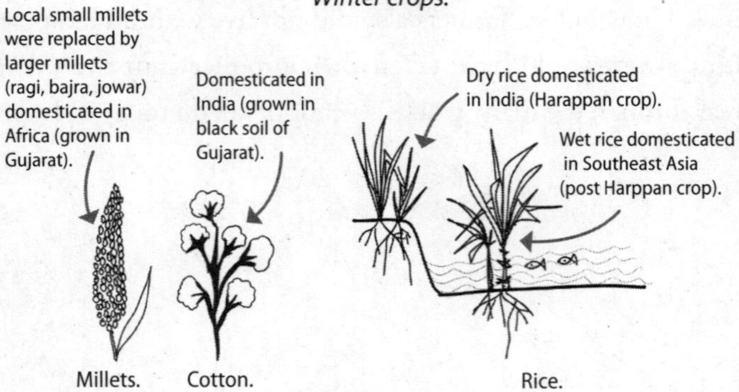

Summer crops.
- Millets. Local small millets were replaced by larger millets (ragi, bajra, jowar) domesticated in Africa (grown in Gujarat).
- Cotton. Domesticated in India (grown in black soil of Gujarat).
- Rice. Dry rice domesticated in India (Harappan crop). Wet rice domesticated in Southeast Asia (post Harppan crop).

Ahimsa

40. Farming

One reason why the Indus river basin, rather than the Ganga river basin, became the first site of major settlements in India, may be the relative softness of soil, which did not need iron ploughs. Also the region did not have as many dense forests.

The Indus Valley was home to many farmers who grew:
- ▶ Summer crops (millets such as ragi, bajra, jowar and cotton) in the monsoon, in Gujarat, and winter crops (wheat, barley) after the monsoon, in Punjab and Haryana.
- ▶ Various kinds of oilseeds (sesame, mustard), vegetables (like brinjal), fruits (like mango and banana) and various spices (turmeric, ginger, garlic).
- ▶ Flax (for linseed oil and linen fibre), cotton (for cottonseed oil and cotton fibre) and jute.

They could grow multiple crops in the same field—cereals in one direction, pulses in another, as revealed by the ploughed field found by archaeologists in Kalibangan, Rajasthan.

Farmers existed before the Harappan cities rose and remained after the Harappan cities fell. They probably never lived in the cities but in neighbouring villages. They lived in houses made of reeds and mud, plastered with dung, as people did until recent times.

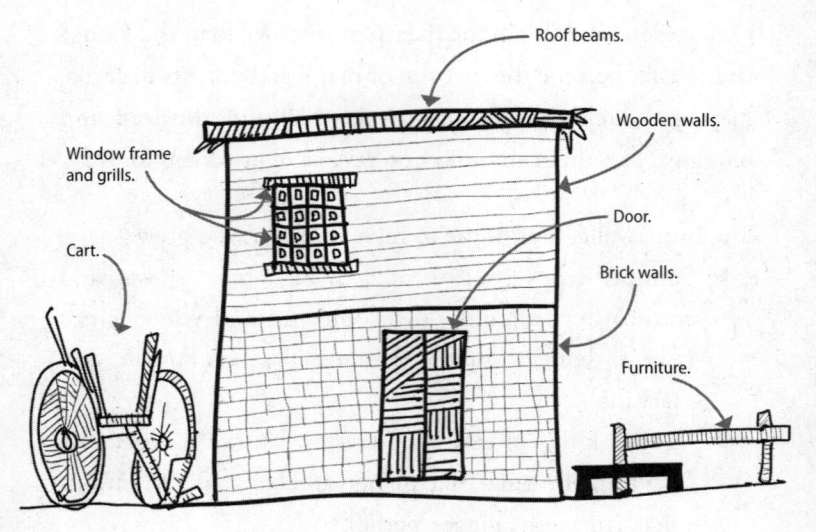

- Roof beams.
- Wooden walls.
- Window frame and grills.
- Door.
- Cart.
- Brick walls.
- Furniture.

Wood in a Harappan city house.

- Sumerian man seated on high stool or chair.
- Indus man seated on low stool.

Furniture.

114   *Ahimsa*

41. Wood Work

Sumerian records refer to timber imported from Meluhha. The famous signboard of Dholavira was made fixing white gypsum pieces to a wooden board. There are grand halls in Mohenjo-daro that are 26 metres in length. Since wooden rafters can stretch only 4-5 metres, this hall must have at least four wooden pillars in five rows (twenty in all). All this indicates that wood—though invisible now—was an integral part of Harappan cities.

The base of Harappan houses was made of bricks. But over this was a wooden superstructure. Wood was used to make pillars, beams, roof, walls, floors of upper levels, doors, windows and ladders. Instead of metal nails, wooden pegs and interlocking wood technology was used. The best wood for this would have been deodar and rosewood (sheesham) from the northern Himalayan forests.

Carpenters made wooden carts, with wooden wheels, which also served as the potter's wheel, wooden furniture like the low stool on which a yogi always sits, boxes for transport and even coffins for the dead. Wood carvers made tools such as ploughs for farmers, spindles and looms for weavers, pegs, spoons, cups, churns and plates for daily domestic use. For this they would have used local wood like neem, palm, acacia and jujube.

Single chamber open kiln.

Harappan man next to a double-chamber closed kiln.

Material	Melting or hardening temperature in degrees Celsius
Tin	232
Lead	327
Gemstone oxidation	400-800
Silver	960
Bronze (copper plus tin)	980
Gold	1064
Copper	1083
Faience	900-1100
Stoneware	1300 (Achieved in Harappan sites)
Iron	1583 (not achieved in Harappan sites, achieved in post-Harappan Ganga river basin sites)

42. Pyro-technology

The Harappans were famous for pyro-technology i.e., their knowledge of fire and ability to create kilns that could produce very high temperatures. This is why they could:

- ▶ Bake bricks, pots and toys.
- ▶ Create glazed, coloured pottery (faience) by baking a mixture of sand and resins at high temperatures.
- ▶ Produce stoneware bangles by heating clay mixed with resin at high temperatures.
- ▶ Harden and change the colours of soft stone (steatite). Special steatite from the Hazara region was used to make seals, which turned white on heating. Other steatite, from other locations, turned black or brown on heating.
- ▶ Heat semi-precious stones (chalcedony) to give them colour and turn them into agate (multi-coloured) and carnelian (red).
- ▶ Smelt copper, tin, lead, gold and silver.
- ▶ Make bronze tools.

These were done in different parts of the city. Some were done outside the city walls to prevent pollution. As per one theory, widespread use of this technology, to meet market demands for its specialized products, led to deforestation and contributed to the end of the civilization.

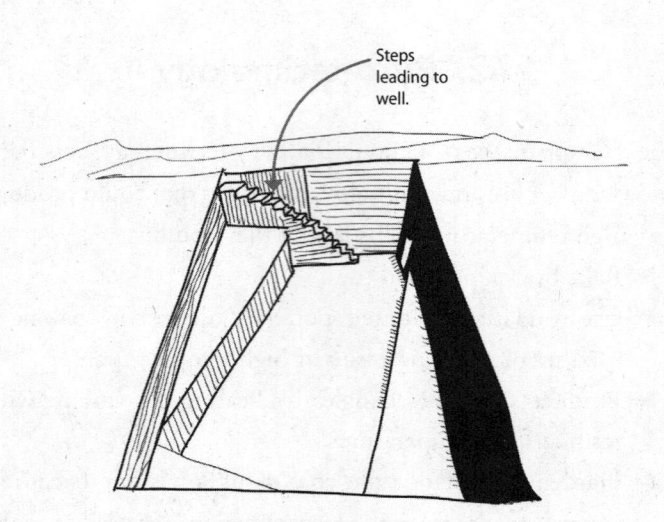

Rock-cut reservoir of Dholavira.

Dholavira gatehouse in Kutch.

43. Stone Work

Harappans in the 'wet' zone cities worked with hard stones, soft stones and coloured stones—all obtained from faraway 'dry' zones.

- ▶ Hard stones obtained from hills at least 200 km from the river were used to make grinding stones, which were essential in kitchens for making flour and pounding spices. The best varieties came from Aravalli.
- ▶ Banded limestone from Kutch was used to make ringstones, which were piled up to make pillars. These were exported from Dholavira to cities in Sindh and Punjab.
- ▶ Chert stones from Sindh's Rohri hills were used to create long and sharp blades that were very popular in Harappan cities.
- ▶ Extremely hard stone tools were made for drilling beads.
- ▶ Soft stone (steatite) was used to make seals and jewellery like beads and bangles. When fired, soft stone would become hard and take different colours. Soft stone was also used to make statues like the 'priest-king' statue.
- ▶ Coloured stones were used, and fired in kilns, to make beads.

Harappans were the first to create rock-cut water reservoirs in Dholavira. Here, the entire city is made of stone, not brick, as stone was easily available.

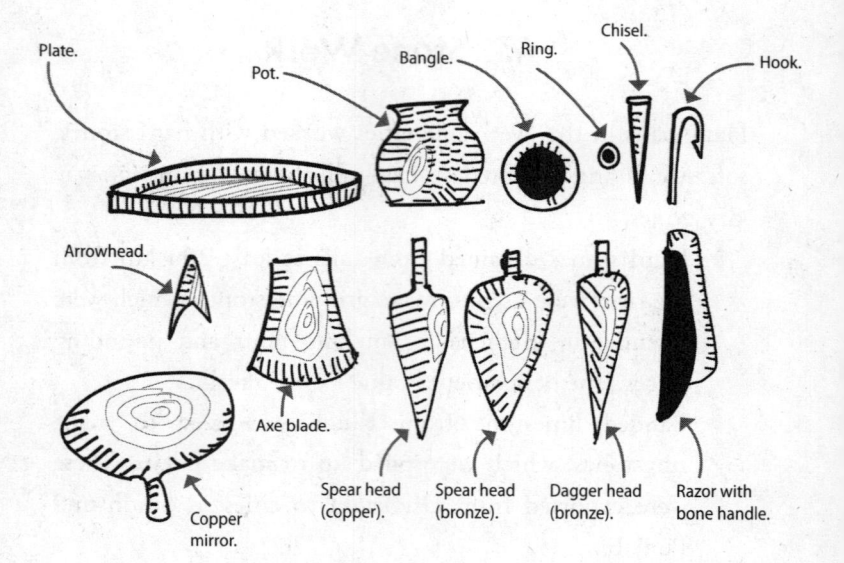

Metal objects.

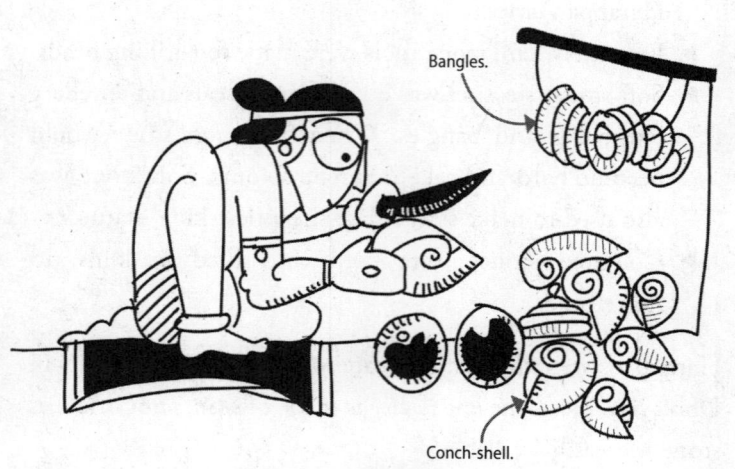

Artisan using bronze blade to cut conch shell to make bangles.

Ahimsa

44. Metal Work

The Harappan made objects with lead, silver, gold, copper and bronze, but not iron. Silver and gold were used for jewellery but were relatively rare. Copper was widely used, and there was some bronze—not very common as tin was not easily available. While craftsmen lived in cities of the 'wet zone', the metal ingots were brought from faraway 'dry' zones. Metal was extracted near the mines itself.

Metal	Source	Finished goods
Copper	Aravalli	Jewellery, mirrors, weighing pans, weapons, utensils and tools
Arsenic	Aravalli	For bronze alloy (more common, but poor quality)
Tin	Imported via Oxus	For bronze alloy (less common, but better quality)
Bronze		Jewellery, mirrors, weapons, utensils, tools, and statues using lost wax technique (mostly exported)
Lead	Aravalli	Beads
Silver	Imported via Mesopotamia	Jewellery (beads, bangles, rings)
Gold	River-panning in Himalayas or imported via Mesopotamia	Jewellery (tiny quantities compared to copper)

Knowledge

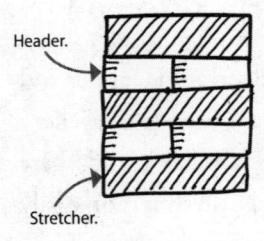

English mason style of bricklaying.

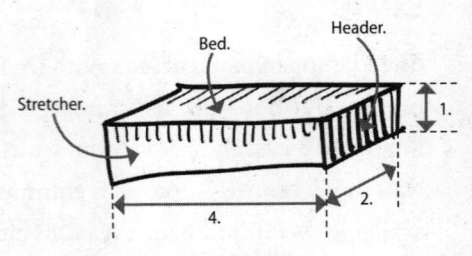

Brick proportions.

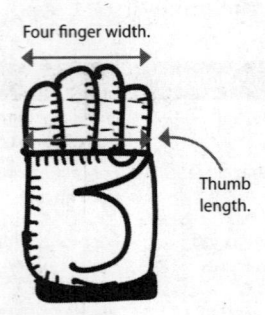

Hand measures.

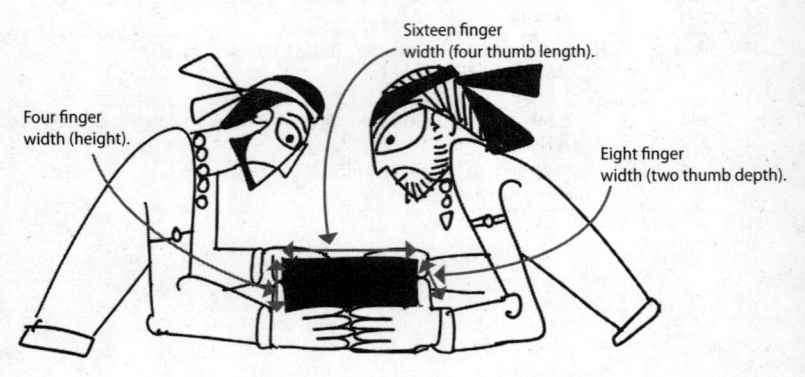

Brick-making using hand to get perfect proportion without use of any mould.

45. Brick-making

Harappan sites are famous for bricks made from the alluvial clay found in river banks. They were different from the bricks used in Mesopotamia.

- ▶ Mesopotamian bricks mixed clay with straw to give it tensile strength. This was not done in the Indus region.
- ▶ Harappan bricks were standardized (4:2:1). Initially this was done using fingers: four finger width, then eight finger width, then sixteen finger width. Later moulds were used.
- ▶ Harappan bricks were often baked in kilns to ensure that they withstood the rains and floods. This was not done in Mesopotamia.

Harappan bricks were made in vast quantities. These were used for building platforms on which the settlements stood; walled enclosures for the settlements; walls for houses and halls; floors of bathing platforms; lining of wells and reservoirs; lining of drains; paving streets.

One wall in Harappa that is 1,800 metres long would have taken about 1,500 people four months to build. This would have been done after the monsoons, when the clay was soft. These walls would need replacement every hundred years or so. So brick-making was an industrial, communal activity.

Basket-maker seated on a reed mat.

Winnowing fan.

46. Baskets

People knew how to weave plant fibres even before they figured out how to make pots. Plant fibres of reed, grass, palm, bamboo, jute and flax were used to make mats, baskets and winnowing fans in the Greater Indus Region as in other river civilizations.

- ▶ Mats were used for sitting and lying on. They were used as curtains on door and window frames.
- ▶ Winnowing fans were used in the fields to separate grain from chaff, using the wind.
- ▶ Baskets were used to collect food.
- ▶ Early pots were made by lining baskets with clay and firing them.
- ▶ Reed mats were also used to wrap the dead during burial and funeral rituals.

Even today, mats, winnowing fans and baskets are considered sacred and used in rituals. Filled with grain and fruits, a basket symbolizes the goddess in many local traditions.

Potter at work.

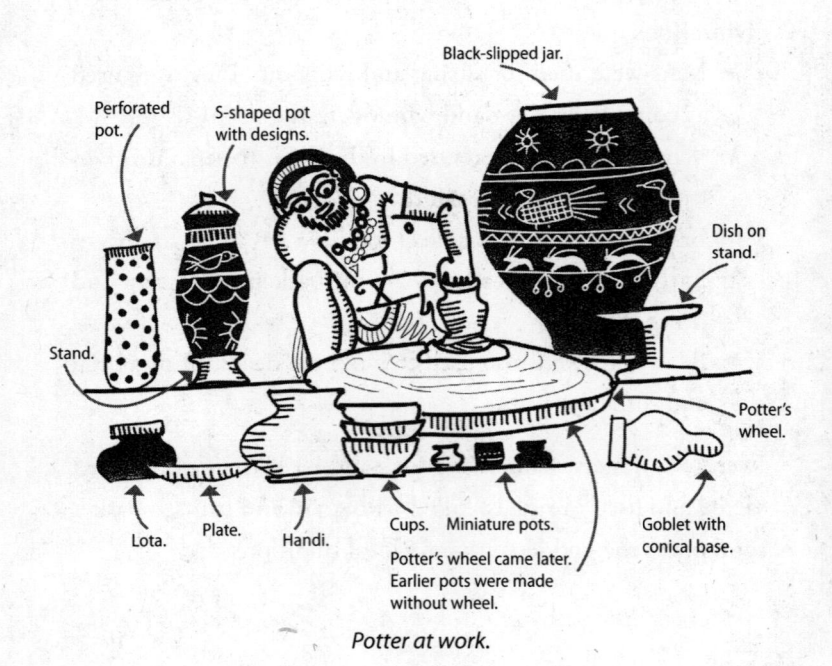

Labels: Perforated pot. S-shaped pot with designs. Black-slipped jar. Dish on stand. Stand. Potter's wheel. Lota. Plate. Handi. Cups. Miniature pots. Goblet with conical base.

Potter's wheel came later. Earlier pots were made without wheel.

Ahimsa

47. Pottery

Pots are used for cooking and storing food; to store goods such as bangles, beads, jewellery; and to bury the dead, or their bones and ash. Besides the famous rimmed handi, lota and thali, there were other pots that are typically Harappan, which we do not see as often today.

- ▶ The giant black-slipped (black outer coat) pot, a metre tall, that was used mostly for exporting goods on boats to faraway Oman. These were built in three parts: the base, the centre and the rim.
- ▶ The painted S-shaped jars 50 cm tall, that look like the Islamic 'surai', different from the more globular and radial 'kumbha' preferred in Hindu rituals.
- ▶ Cone-shaped goblets, that could be stacked easily during storage and transport, and driven into earth, or between wooden racks on ships, to prevent them from tumbling. There were special potholder rings for these pots too.
- ▶ Perforated jars (20 cm) for making beer or cheese.
- ▶ Dishes on stands (30 cm), to keep food away from ants, and maybe used in rituals.
- ▶ Miniature pots (5 cm) either used for storing cosmetics or as toys.
- ▶ Clay oil lamps with a depression for the wick.

Multicoloured pots were more widespread before the rise of urban settlements.

Beads that have same colour as semi-precious stones so served as imitations:
blue (lapis lazuli), red (carnelian), multicoloured (agate).

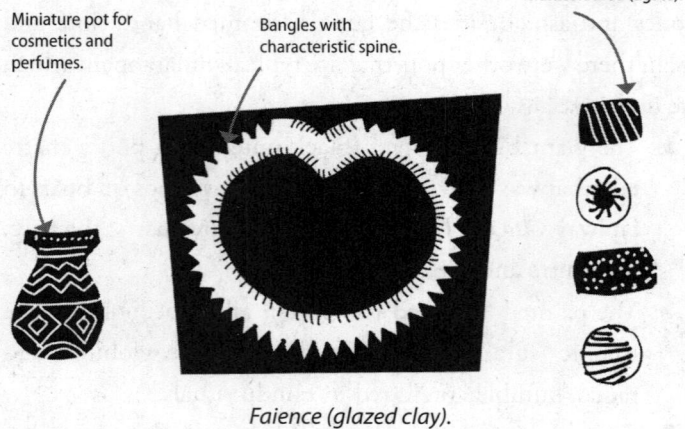

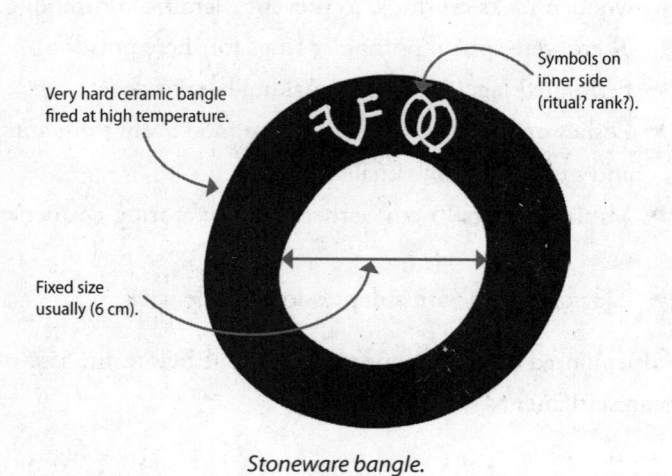

Miniature pot for cosmetics and perfumes.

Bangles with characteristic spine.

Faience (glazed clay).

Very hard ceramic bangle fired at high temperature.

Symbols on inner side (ritual? rank?).

Fixed size usually (6 cm).

Stoneware bangle.

48. Faience

Originally people made beads using natural stones: lapis lazuli, turquoise, agate, vesuvianite.

But over time, Harappans began using faience technology that allowed them to glaze and colour clay. Quartz sand was mixed with resin and various colouring agents and heated at different temperatures to create glazed objects. These had the same colour as natural stones. This 'imitation' was easy to manufacture. So, many of the beads we see in Harappa are not made of naturally coloured rocks; they are glazed and coloured clay beads, mostly blue-green, produced with faience technology.

Besides beads, this technique was employed to make buttons, toys and tiny pots that were used to store cosmetics—like black surma for the eyes, red ochre for lips and cheeks, and maybe cinnabar for sindoor.

Harappan technology disappeared after the urban phase, but new technology appeared independently, centuries later, and is still found in meenakari ornaments of India today.

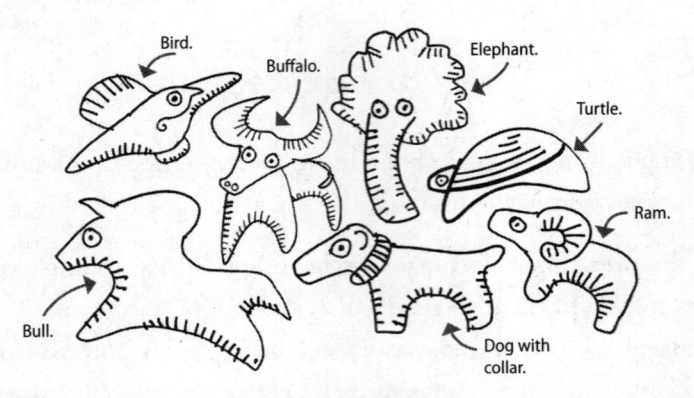

Animal figurines.

- Bird.
- Buffalo.
- Elephant.
- Turtle.
- Ram.
- Dog with collar.
- Bull.

Game boards.

- Board from Dholavira has same design as board game from Ur.
- Dice.
- Board game pieces (some assume these are 'linga' representations).

Mobile toys.

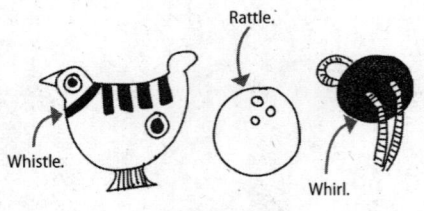

- Moving head.
- Wheeled toy.
- Tops.

Musical toys.

- Whistle.
- Rattle.
- Whirl.

130   Ahimsa

49. Toy-making

Harappans loved making toys using wood as well as clay, faience, ivory and bone. These were certainly for children but could as well be used as votive offerings in shrines, as they still are in many Hindu rituals.

The toys include figures of different animals: tigers, rhinoceroses, elephants, unicorns, lions (rare), sheep, goats, dogs, parrots, pigeons, partridges, peacocks, chickens and pheasants.

Some toys have multiple mobile units. For example, the wheels and the oxen of a cart could be separately attached. You could move the neck and limbs of animals. Flutes shaped like birds could be used to make bird sounds.

Clay masks were created for use in theatre. Tops were created to whirl.

There were also games—the pawns, the counting board, the dice, the game board. What kind of games did they play? We do not know. The Harappan dice were different from the modern ones in that they may not always have six sides and the sum of opposite sides was not seven. This makes them different from standardized modern dice.

Drumming to woo tiger (Harappan clay tablet).

Musicians (speculative).

132   *Ahimsa*

50. Musicians

The Harappans made music. The seals reveal that they danced and played the drums and pipe. But the musical instruments have not survived as they were mostly made of reeds, wood and leather. Strings were made using animal guts. They may have been familiar with musical stones. Incidentally, the oldest musical stones (lithophones) have been found in Odisha, dated to 5000 BC.

We can get some idea of what Harappans used as musical instruments by studying Sumerian art and information provided on Sumerian scripts, especially when related to Meluhha. The music in Sumer had seven notes. Later Tamil Sangam poetry (AD 100) does refer to seven notes.

Like Sumerians, the Harappans may have used:
- ▶ Stringed instruments like harps and lutes.
- ▶ Percussion instruments like pots and drums.
- ▶ Wind instruments like flutes made of reed and bamboo, whistles, conch-shell and other trumpets.
- ▶ Clappers and rattles made of terracotta and stones.

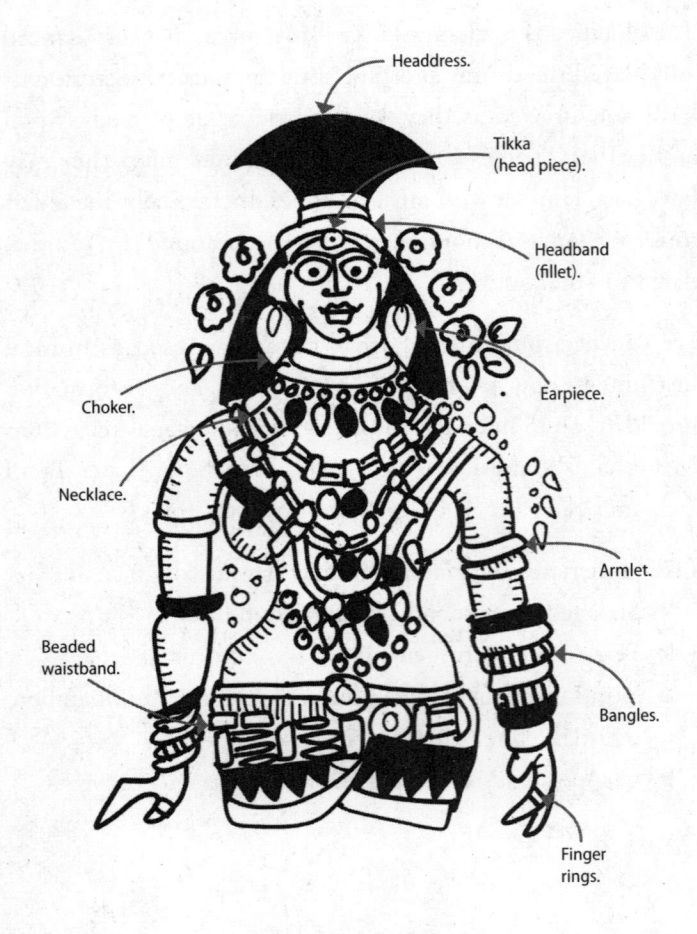

Bejewelled woman.

51. Jewellery

Harappans loved jewellery. Both men and women adorned their bodies with many ornaments. Ornaments were used to show clan identity as well as marital, social and religious status. Jewellery, not seals, were taken to the grave. Jewellery was made using precious materials (fired stones, metal, ivory) and also cheaper material (terracotta, faience, steatite). Every part of the body was adorned.

- ▶ Bangles were popular, worn by men and women as armlets and bracelets and to adorn various hairstyles.
- ▶ Beads were strung around the head, neck and waist. They were also used to adorn the hair.
- ▶ Rings were used for fingers, toes and ankles.
- ▶ The tikka for the head, still used by women in Rajasthan, Punjab and Haryana, has been found on Harappan figurines.
- ▶ Figurines showed that women wore elaborate headdresses while men had bands around their heads and their hair worn in buns.
- ▶ In many regions, pierced ears and nose identify people as members of a community. Did Harappans pierce their ears and noses as Indians do today? It is not very clear.

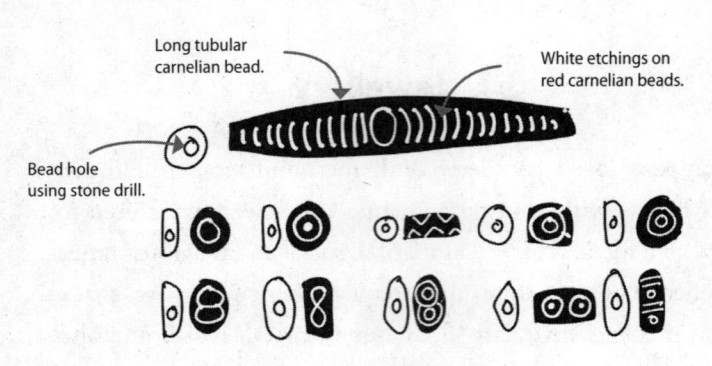

Beads.

Bead-maker of Harappa.

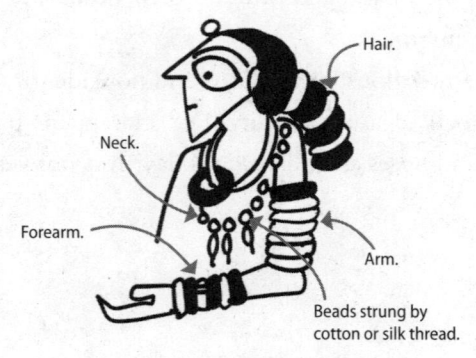

Bangles worn in different ways.

Ahimsa

52. Bangles and Beads

Two pieces of jewellery need specific attention, for their presence around the ancient world is an indicator of the craftsmanship of the Harappans: bangles and beads.

- ▶ No other civilization produced bangles on the scale the Harappans did, and it remains an integral part of jewellery today, as indicators of marital status or as offerings to the gods. From the richest to the poorest, people wear bangles: made of metal, clay, glass or shell. Two types of bangles that Harappans made were unique. They did not know glass, but they made stoneware bangles, which were ceramic and made very hard by firing clay mixed with resin at very high temperatures. Then there were conch-shell ones made by cutting conch shells found along the Gujarat coast. These were rare commodities, much sought in Mesopotamia.

- ▶ Beads that came from Harappa were unique. Not only did they have exclusive access to lapis lazuli (blue stone) and vesuvianite (green stone), but they could also make long tubular beads of carnelian (red stone). Only Harappans knew how to drill holes in such long beads. And they could etch white designs on the red carnelian beads. For this, they employed a special technique that involved painting beads with a plant juice before firing them. This could not be imitated by faience bead makers, and so were much in demand.

Woman with flat headdress.

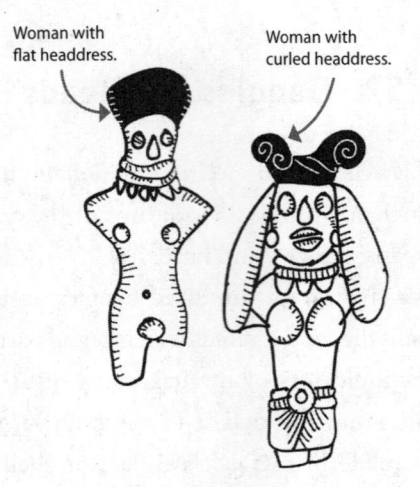

Woman with curled headdress.

Leather hood.

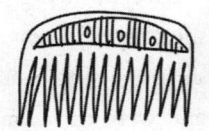

Ivory comb.

Bone inlay.

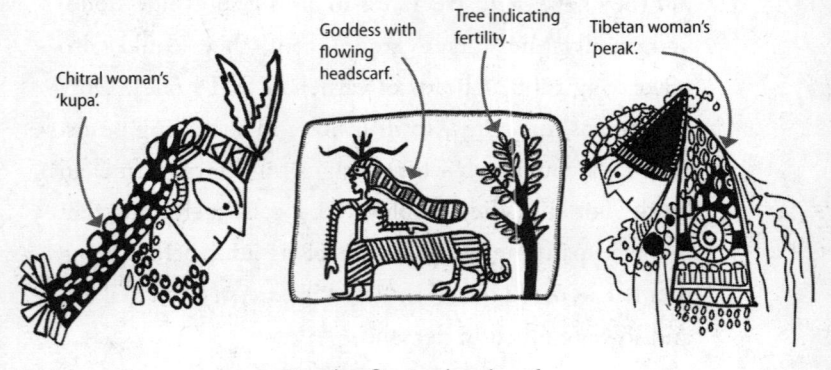

Chitral woman's 'kupa'.

Goddess with flowing headscarf.

Tree indicating fertility.

Tibetan woman's 'perak'.

Leather flowing headscarf.

53. Leather, Ivory, Bone, Horn

Harappan cities had craftsmen who worked with leather, ivory, bone and horn, obtained from elephants, cattle, buffaloes, sheep and goats. Of these only objects made of ivory, bone and horn survive. These were used to make various tools and jewellery.

- Buttons.
- Talismans.
- Beads.
- Combs.
- Pins.
- Hooks.
- Inlaid pieces used in games, furniture and jewellery.

Many artifacts have been found in the Oxus civilization. Most of the objects were items of daily use and not for artwork. These were in demand in the elite communities.

Leather may have been used in the making of the elaborate hats that the Harappans wore as indicated by the figurines. The leather may also have been used to make a headdress known as 'perak', worn by Ladakhi women in the Himalayan region to protect the back of their necks. These were made of leather studded with lapis lazuli and turquoise. A similar headdress, made of wool, studded with cowrie shells, is worn by the Kalash women of Chitral, Pakistan, and called 'kupa'.

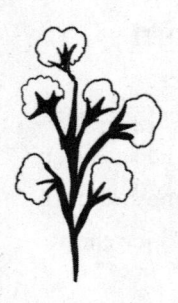

Cotton plant.

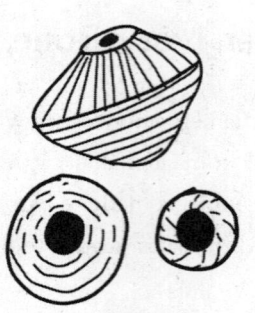

Terracotta spindle whorls.

Khes weave found in Sindh and Punjab today.

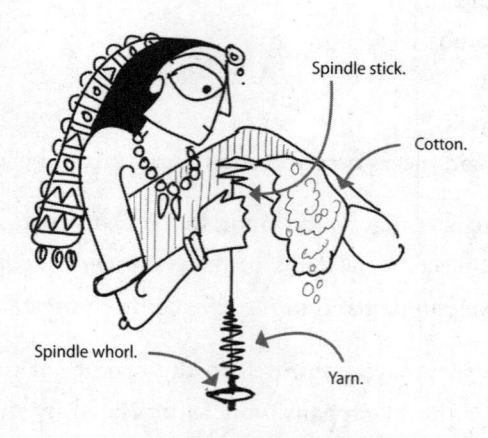

Harappan woman spinning yarn.

- Spindle stick.
- Cotton.
- Spindle whorl.
- Yarn.

Jute cloth used to seal pots.

- Jute cloth.
- Flax thread.
- Clay sealing.
- Pot.

54. Textile Work

People of the southern Indus region grew cotton and jute in summer, while those in the northern Indus region grew flax (linseed) in winter. Seeds of cotton and flax were used to make oil. This oil was used for lamps. Cotton flowers, and the extract from stalks of flax and jute, were spun into threads using spindles. This was woven into cloth, which was then coloured using plant dyes such as indigo (blue), turmeric (yellow), madder (red) and catechu (brown).

- ▶ Coarse cloth and ropes were used as packing material, and for making sails of boats.
- ▶ Fine cloth was worn, probably as unstitched garments.

Finely woven and brightly dyed cotton cloth was probably a major export to Mesopotamia. Fibre, like wood, is not easily found in archaeological sites. But scientists have found the fibre within beads, impressions of cloth on clay, hundreds of spindle whorls and seeds of cotton and indigo. Together these indicate the existence of a textile industry—a major Harappan export. The famous 'granaries' of Mohenjo-daro were probably workshops where fabric was dyed.

Silk thread has also been found. This was obtained from local wild silk moths (tussar). These were not woven into fabric. The thread was used to string beads.

Knowledge

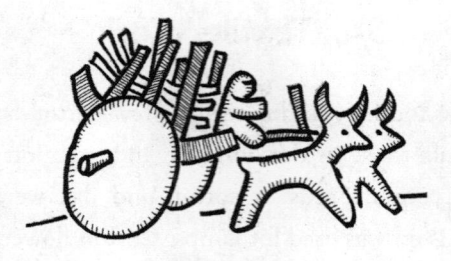

Cart figurine.

Man with shoulder yoke.

Goat as pack animal.

55. Carts and Transport

The Harappans used carts to transport goods. This is easy when the ground is flat and hard—in winter and summer. But not during the rains or floods, when the riverbanks are soft. The cities were paved with bricks. Drains ensured there was no flooding of streets. Bins were located to prevent accumulation of waste.

The wagons had solid wheels. These would make the wagon heavy. Only oxen could pull these heavy wagons. In Harappa there are small toys showing wagons with solid carts and bulls. Images of bull-drawn wagons are found in the Oxus civilization. Solid-wheel wagons were found in burial sites in the Ganga river basin dated to 1000 BC, at Sanuali.

That the Harappan script has many symbols based on shoulder-yokes suggests that this piece of equipment was commonly used to transport goods, much like it is today in many places across South and Southeast Asia.

But carts would be useless on mountain paths. Here, goats were used. Goats can carry about 20 per cent of their body weight and may have been used to carry goods like stones and metal ingots. Elephants may have been domesticated and used in the transport of timber.

Donkeys from Egypt, horses from Eurasia and double-humped camels from Central Asia came much later, when the Harappan cities were long gone.

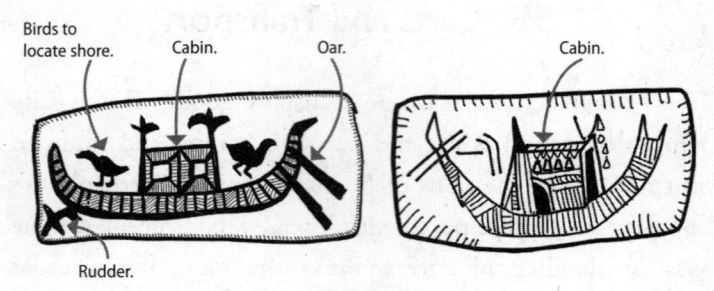

Indus images of boats.

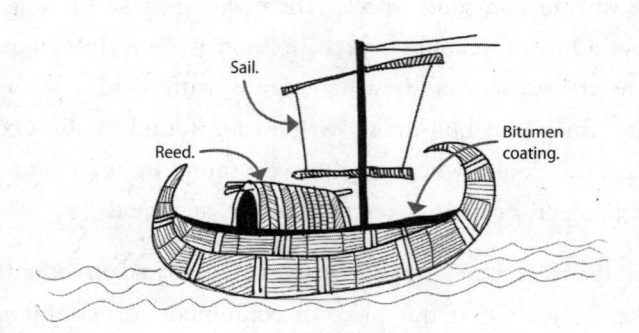

Reed boat.

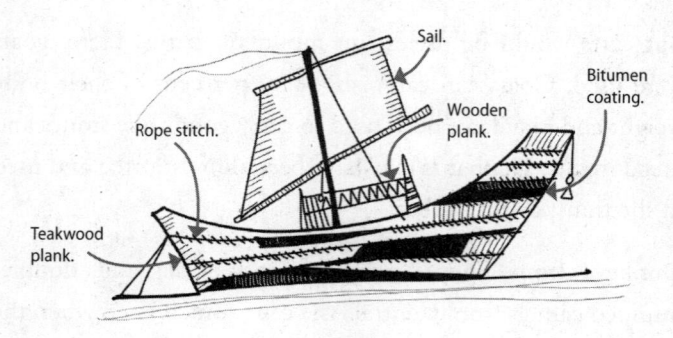

Flat wooden boat.

56. Shipping

Boats took goods up and down the Indus river, and along the coast, even across the gulf to Magan—a distance covered in two days if the monsoon wind-power was harnessed. This explains the intense trading relationship from Meluhha to Magan, across the strait.

Harappan seals show images of reed boats and flat-based wooden boats. Shipbuilders would have used water-resistant teak from Gujarat to make flat-based wooden boats with masts and square sails, to travel with monsoon winds. The planks may have been 'stitched' and made waterproof using fish oil, special plant 'dammar' resin and bitumen. The shape of the sails was probably square to push ships ahead of the wind; triangular ones that allow ships to sail also towards the wind were invented later.

Ships mostly sailed along the coast; sailing on open seas was a risk. Availability of long copper fishing hooks indicates some did venture farther out. If the ship drifted too far into sea, away from the shoreline, the sailors would release birds (crows, doves) that would fly in the direction of the shore. A hymn in the Rig Veda refers to this practice: 'He, who knows the path of the birds flying through the air; he, abiding in the ocean, knows (also) the course of ships.' This is yet another example of Harappan memory making its way into Aryan poetry.

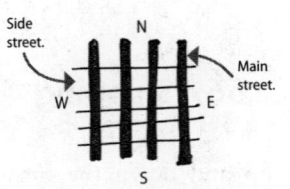

Typical city orientation.

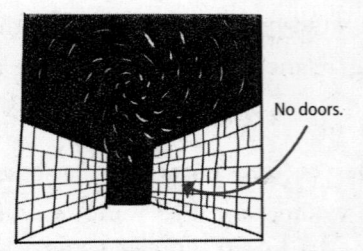

Main street aligned to north-south. Mostly wide enough for one cart, so one-way traffic.

Side lane aligned with east and west.

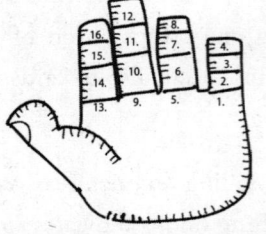

Finger counting using sixteen base.

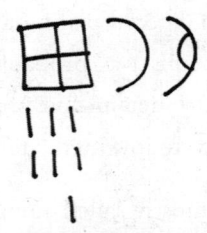

Marks that may have been used for counting.

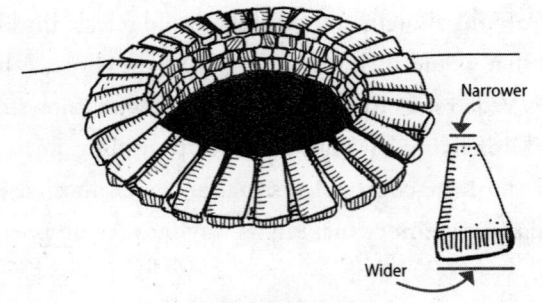

Trapezoid bricks for wells.

57. Mathematics

The Harappans, like most ancient people, had a practical knowledge of mathematics and geometry, which they developed as per need. This was evident in:

- ▶ Standard urban planning using grid-like streets, mapped along the cardinal directions, intersecting at right angles.
- ▶ Designing proportioned enclosures either as rectangles or parallelograms.
- ▶ Understanding proportion and standardization in the design of bricks for houses (4:2:1) and trapezoid bricks for wells.
- ▶ Understanding of principles of displacement and retention in water reservoirs.
- ▶ Understanding of volume, slope and density to manage a city's drainage system.
- ▶ Standard use of weights and measures using seeds.
- ▶ Standard counting system using fingers.
- ▶ Understanding of accounting and book-keeping for managing, rationing and distribution of grain, as well as for taxation, credit and debt.
- ▶ Harappans were probably familiar with the gnomon or sun-stick. In the city of Dholavira, located on the Tropic of Cancer, astronomers have found two circular rooms that could have served as an observatory.

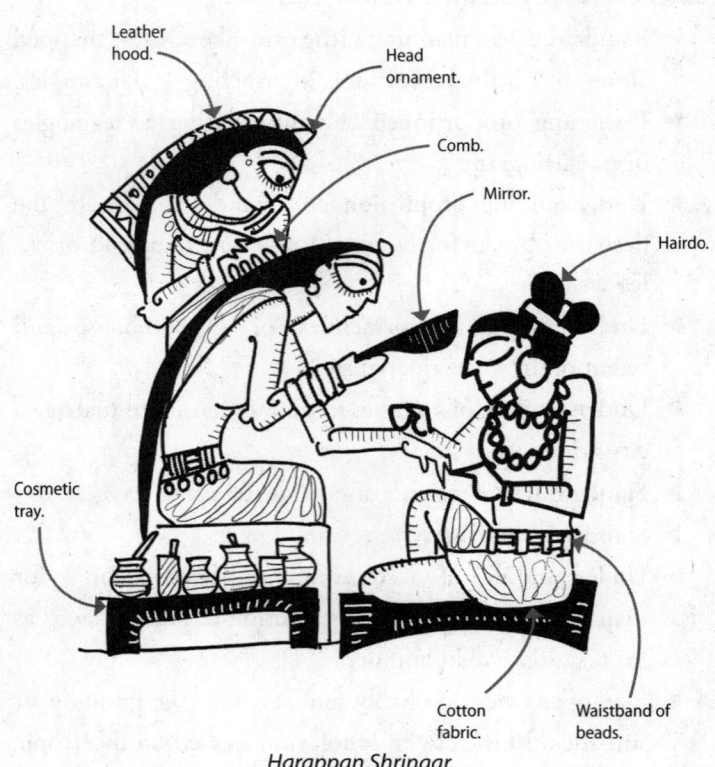

Harappan Shringar.

58. Fashion and Cosmetics

The Harappans were a pragmatic people. All their artifacts suggests a rather utilitarian mindset. But they seemed to be fashion-conscious and familiar with cosmetics. Besides jewellery, they were particular about painting their bodies and styling their hair.

- Mirrors found at burial sites indicate the importance given to grooming.
- At Banawali, in Haryana, there are suggestions that people used plant-based detergent products such as reetha, shikakai and amla for washing their hair and body.
- Cosmetic boxes have been found, which suggests lamp black, mixed with ghee, was used to darken the eye. These were placed in tiny containers, and there are ivory sticks that were used for application.
- Cinnabar was used to colour lips and cheeks and in the parting of the hair as sindoor.
- Many combs have been found, made of bone and ivory.
- Tweezers were used to pull out unwanted hair.
- Ear scoops were used to clear the ears.
- Small razors were used to remove body hair.
- Sharp toothpicks have also been found.
- Tiny pots may have been used to store various aromatic oils, resins, perfumes and pastes.

Maybe the idea of shringar, preparing the body aesthetically, has its roots in Harappa.

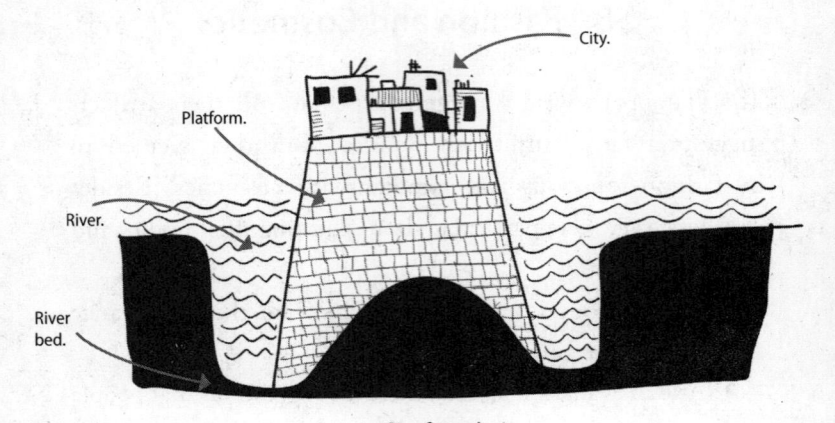

City foundation.

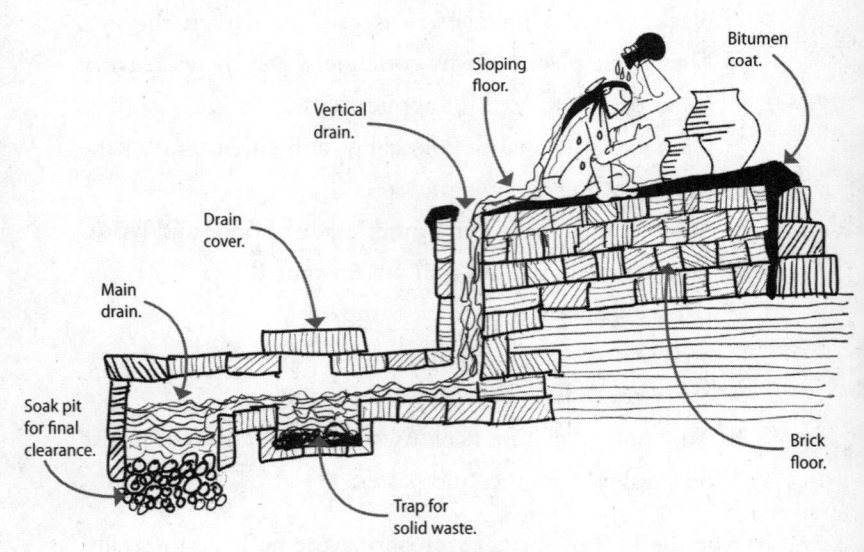

Private bathing platform.

59. Architecture and Water Engineering

Harappan cities were built on huge brick and earth platforms to protect against flooding. They had a clear grid of streets within a rectangular perimeter. This indicates the presence of good architects and engineers.

New structures were built on old houses. That is why all houses were at different levels. Gated enclosures at higher levels were those of older and more prosperous communities.

Water management was key.
- Brick-lined wells were used in Mohenjo-daro, one in each housing area, to get to the ground water.
- Water reservoirs of Dholavira, Lothal and Harappa were used to harvest rain and river water during the monsoons.

Drainage of sewage was key too—with terracotta pipes and bricks laid out in a slope to collect water by channelling it into larger drains. These drains had covers as well as pits for collecting solid waste. Household toilets had soak-pits. Streets had storm sewers to clear water.

This required continuous maintenance. Was this managed by a community (jati) with its own seal? Did this community enable craftsmen to live in enclosed and regulated workshops, without having to leave the walled compounds to get water, bathe or use the latrine?

Knowledge

Harappan market.

60. Internal Trade

Compared to Egypt and Sumer, the Harappan civilization occupied a wider space, over a million square kilometres, and had a more diverse ecosystem. It had over five major urban centres, each occupying an area of more than 100 hectares, with a population of over 20,000 people.

The cities were famous for the supply of certain raw materials and certain finished products. They probably used cowries as currency. These were all interconnected, part of a supply-chain regulated by people who used unicorn seals.

- ▶ Harappa was the most important city regulating goods (lapiz lazuli, turquoise, steatite, tin, timber) coming from the northern mountains via the Gomal and Khyber passes.
- ▶ Mohenjo-daro was at the crossroads of the north-south river route and east-west land routes passing through the Rohri hills and Bolan Pass.
- ▶ Ganweriwala controlled trade over the now-dry Saraswati river.
- ▶ Rakhigarhi was the easternmost city that controlled access to the Aravallis.
- ▶ Lothal was the site controlling access to precious chalcedony (agate, carnelian) and conch shells from the Arabian Sea.
- ▶ Dholavira was highly fortified, and controlled the coastal shipping lanes.

Meluhhan translator Shu-ilishu in Sumer.

Water buffalo imported from Meluhha.

61. External Trade

We do not know what the Harappan people called their land. All we know is that in 2300 BC, the Akkadian kings who ruled Sumer referred to the land as Meluhha. This was written in cuneiform script on clay tablets. Meluhha is thus an exonym, a name given by outsiders. Significantly, even names like 'Hind' and 'Indus' are exonyms given to Indians by Persians and Greeks, around 500 BC.

External trade played a key role in the rise of the Harappan urban ecosystem. Cuneiform tablets in Mesopotamia give the following information:

- Boats from Dilmun (Bahrain), Magan (Oman) and Meluhha (Makran) were docked in ports of the Akkadian empire.
- Shu-ilishu was interpreter of the Meluhhan language.
- Timber came from Meluhha.
- Meluhha's people were considered dark-skinned.
- There is a reference to the 'bird of Meluhha' (chicken or peacock).
- There is reference to a 'red dog of Meluhha' (dhole or Indian wild dog).
- There is even reference to war with Meluhha.

At Oman (Magan), Harappan-style pottery and seals have been found with minor differences. These indicate that a new merchant guild, with Harappan roots, established a base at the Arabian peninsula, controlling the trade to and from Sumer.

Wedge-shaped (cuneiform) script was invented by accountants of Sumer.

Meluhha written in Cuneiform script.

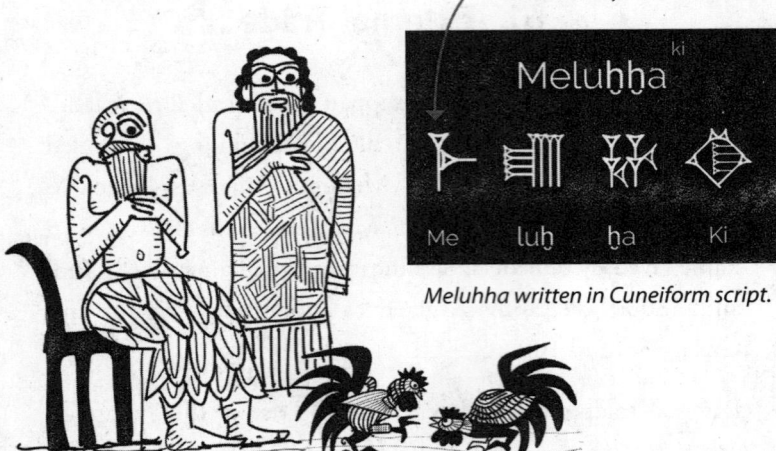

Sumerians watching roosters from Meluhha.

Import from Meluhha	Export to Meluhha
■ Dyed cotton fabrics.	■ Woolen fabrics that Mesopotamia was famous for.
■ Bronze (with tin from Central Asia and copper form Aravallis).	■ Bitumen (for water-proofing baths and bathing platforms).
■ Jewellery (stoneware bangles, necklaces, waistband).	■ Silver, gold from Anatolia.
■ Beads of lapis lazuli (blue stone from Afghanistan), carnelian (red stone from Gujarat), vesuvianite (green stone from Khyber).	■ Incense.
■ Imitation faience ceramic beads.	
■ Conch shells (from Arabian sea).	
■ Ivory and bone inlays.	
■ Timber (cedar, teak, sheesham).	
■ Animals (water buffalo, dog).	
■ Birds (chicken, peacock).	

Ahimsa

62. Import-Export

While Harappan seals and goods have been found in Mesopotamia, Mesopotamian seals and goods are not found in the Greater Indus Region. As Harappan internal trade ensured self-sufficiency, imports were probably commodities not found easily around the Indus.

Harappans seem to have been a rather insular people, avoiding Sumerian influence. Despite long contact, Harappans did not adopt the cuneiform script or a love for luxury. Harappans remained a rather restrained people, more institutional, more collaborative, less violent.

Trade with Sumer was clearly the lifeblood of the Harappan cities. Demand from Sumerian temples for luxury goods and luxury products is what sustained the workshops along the Indus. In 2300 BC, the Sumerian cities were conquered. They became part of the Akkadian empire, but demand for Harappan goods continued. But by 2000 BC, when the Akkadian empire collapsed, Sumerian cities did not function as independent entities. Something changed. Agrarian output fell and focus shifted northwards, up the Euphrates towards Anatolia. New trade routes opened directly with BMAC. The Harappan supply chain was bypassed. Meluhha's unique brand of goods lost relevance. This played a key role in the collapse of the Harappan urban ecosystem.

The Harappan cities had walls, gates and seals to regulate movement of goods.

Standardization

Diversity is inefficient. Businessmen prefer standardization. But standardization takes away freedom. While Mesopotamia witnessed a shift from city-states to empires, the Greater Indus Region witnessed a shift from diverse cultures (vi-yoga) to cities shaped by a standard template (sama-yoga), before returning to diversity (vi-yoga). The period of standardization is called the period of civilization as it is linked with urbanization and permanent structures. This lasted for 700 years, marked by standard city layouts, standard bricks, standard weights, standard designs and common burial and pottery styles. All things foreign were kept out. Restraint and discipline was valorized.

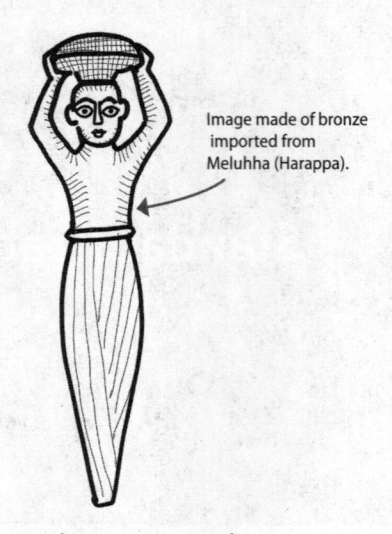

Sumerian king carrying earth for temple construction.

Image made of bronze imported from Meluhha (Harappa).

Strings of beads, imported from Meluhha (Harappa), found in tomb of Sumerian queen.

Sumerian devotee.

Eyes made of lapis lazuli imported from Meluhha (Harappa).

63. Luxury from Meluhha

In Sumerian mythology, gods created humans to do labour. If humans disobeyed, they suffered floods. So everyone in Sumer worked for the gods—even the kings. They dug canals, worked in farms, built temples, and discovered new materials that made their gods happy:

- ▶ Lapis lazuli, a mysterious deep blue stone that came from the east.
- ▶ Tin, also from the east, that turned copper into bronze—an alloy that was easier to melt, less brittle and more resistant to corrosion.

The coast of Meluhha was the source, connected via rivers to faraway mountains. A system of standardization was established to enable a smooth, trustworthy and predictable supply. The sacred nature of the goods explains the obsessive need for control, secrecy and purity. Isolated in compounds, workers needed indoor toilets. Bathing washed away the pollution.

The standardization remained relatively static for 700 years, with hardly any innovation. Unlike Sumerian cities that were highly independent, individualistic, competitive and creative, the Harappan cities were highly institutional and monastic, stifling vibrancy and creativity.

Egyptian pyramids (2500 BC)

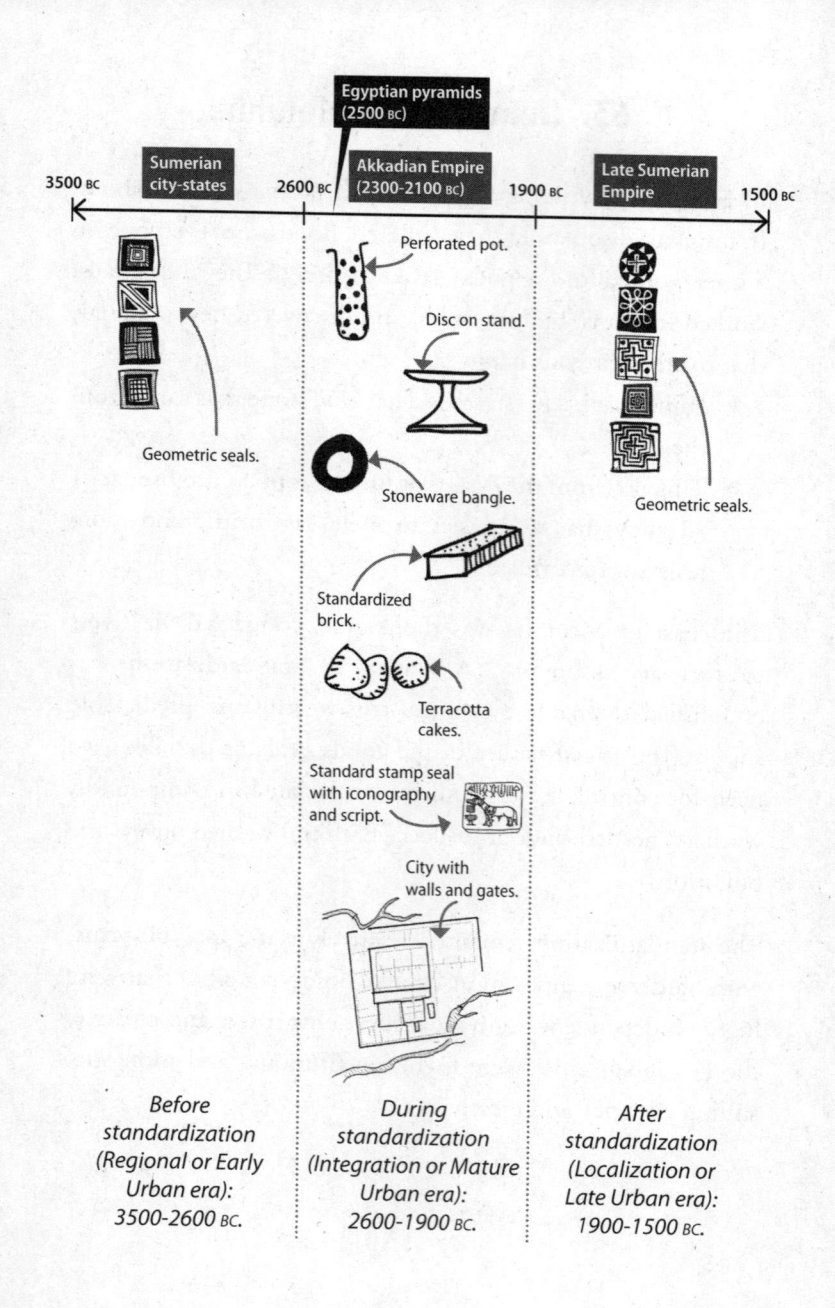

3500 BC — **Sumerian city-states** — 2600 BC — **Akkadian Empire (2300-2100 BC)** — 1900 BC — **Late Sumerian Empire** — 1500 BC

Geometric seals.

Perforated pot.

Disc on stand.

Stoneware bangle.

Standardized brick.

Terracotta cakes.

Standard stamp seal with iconography and script.

City with walls and gates.

Geometric seals.

Before standardization (Regional or Early Urban era): 3500-2600 BC.

During standardization (Integration or Mature Urban era): 2600-1900 BC.

After standardization (Localization or Late Urban era): 1900-1500 BC.

162 Ahimsa

64. Template

The Harappan civilization was twenty times the size of the Egyptian civilization and ten times the size of the Mesopotamian civilization. It was full of small (less than 10 hectares) and large settlements (over 100 hectares) that followed the same rules of standardization that remained in place for at least twenty generations. The template included:

- Standard city layout with platforms, walls, gates, grid-layout, common administrative zone.
- Standard home design, which included indoor plumbing that connected to a city-wide network of drains with traps, sumps and soak-pits.
- Standard seals, made of standard material, using standard manufacturing processes and standard design features.
- Standard script with symbols that provided logistic and fiscal information understood by suppliers, distributors, manufacturers and transporters speaking many languages.
- Standard weights, measures and brick dimensions.
- Standard burial practice.
- Standard pottery style, with black-on-red design.
- Standard production of specialized goods: long, tubular red carnelian beads with white etching, special ceramic stoneware bangles, terracotta cakes used in kilns.

None of these were necessary for survival. So when the old Sumerian culture withered away, so did need for the ritualistic 'standardized' supply-chain.

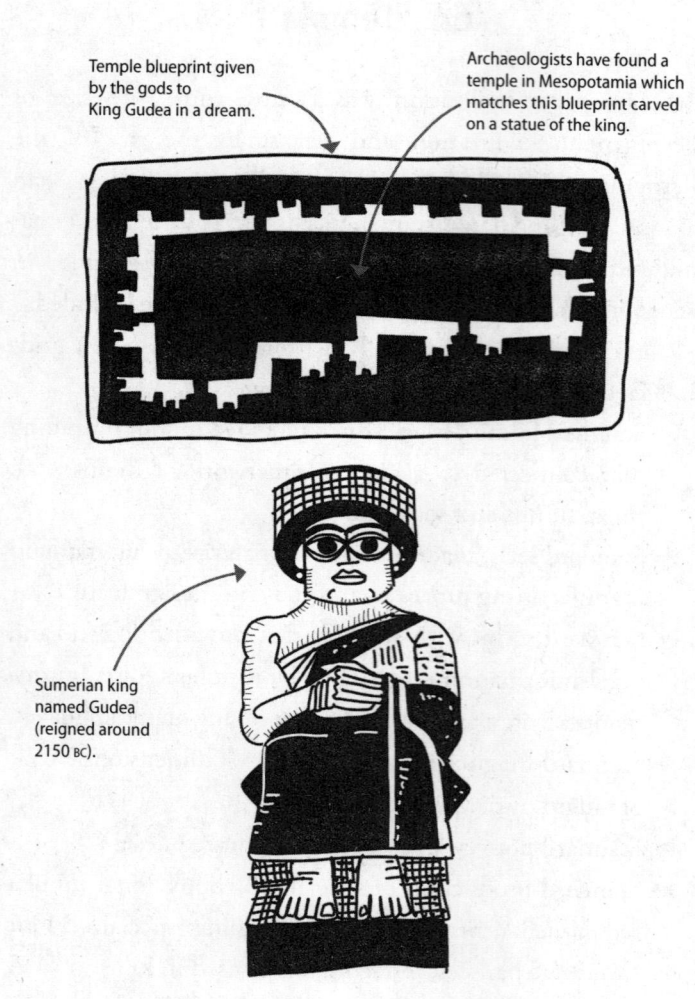

Temple blueprint given by the gods to King Gudea in a dream.

Archaeologists have found a temple in Mesopotamia which matches this blueprint carved on a statue of the king.

Sumerian king named Gudea (reigned around 2150 BC).

Sacred proportions in ancient Sumer.

65. Sacred Proportions

For the Chinese, jade has a special spiritual significance that is lost on Hindus. For Hindus, gold is not just precious; it is also auspicious. The beads of rudraksha are auspicious but not precious. The holiness of cows and impurity of pigs means they will not be consumed, even if it makes economic sense. Beliefs thus shift the material value of commodities. Belief is what increased demand for lapis lazuli and bronze. Belief is what ensured the standardization of Harappa with minimum violence. Some key Harappan beliefs were:

- ▶ The obsession with purity (bathing platforms and drains), simplicity (absence of monumental art, shunning colourful pots and walls) and isolation (more exports than imports, more gates) which indicates that power was linked to restraint and denial.
- ▶ Sumerian temples had fixed proportions that kings claimed were revealed by gods. So the 4:2:1 design of Harappan bricks had special meaning that no one dared challenge. The pragmatic benefits were incidental.

Belief is not measurable so is out of reach of scientists, who tend to be dismissive of the non-measurable realm of emotions and imagination, which are the real driving forces of civilization. Sumerians built monuments because of their myth. Harappans did not build monuments because of their myth.

Entrance into a gated compound.

Reed house outside cities.

166

66. Gated Communities

People speak of 1,500 Harappan sites over 1,000,000 square kilometres. However, these sites rose and fell over 700 years, shifting with shifting river patterns. Many sites were tiny, providing shelter to travelling merchants. Some were feeders to the main cities. At any one time, probably a hundred small sites served the five or six major cities.

These cities followed a standard template of design and process. Homogeneity creates trust. Even today, many trading communities are bound by common religions, common gurus, common temples. In faraway lands, the presence of a familiar culture makes you feel safe.

Only those involved in the production of specialized goods had to live within gated communities, use indoor lavatories and bathe indoor, at least during the production cycle. Their movement was regulated like the movement of raw materials and finished goods. They differentiated themselves from others using clothes and jewellery. The costume made them feel special, different, unique, part of a commune almost, manufacturing goods for the pleasure of gods, an idea that motivated them to stay isolated voluntarily and encourage their children to do so.

However, the farmers, the herders, the fishermen, the miners, were not part of the walled city and its 'sealed' tunnel. Their life remained unchanged with and without the cities.

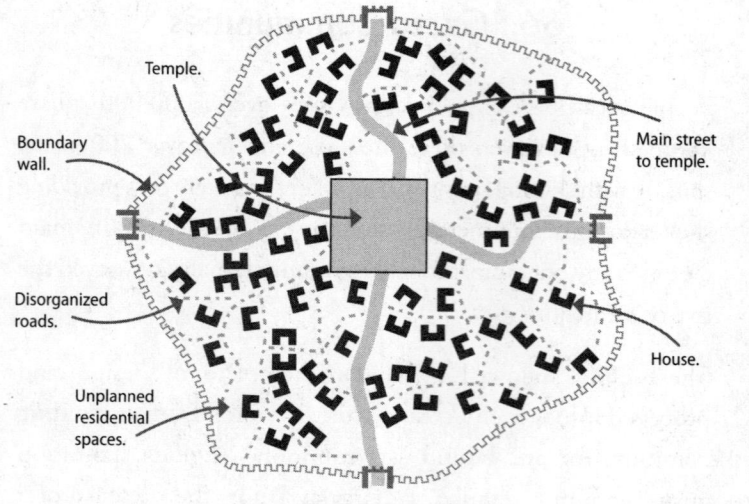

Mesopotamian city (unplanned).

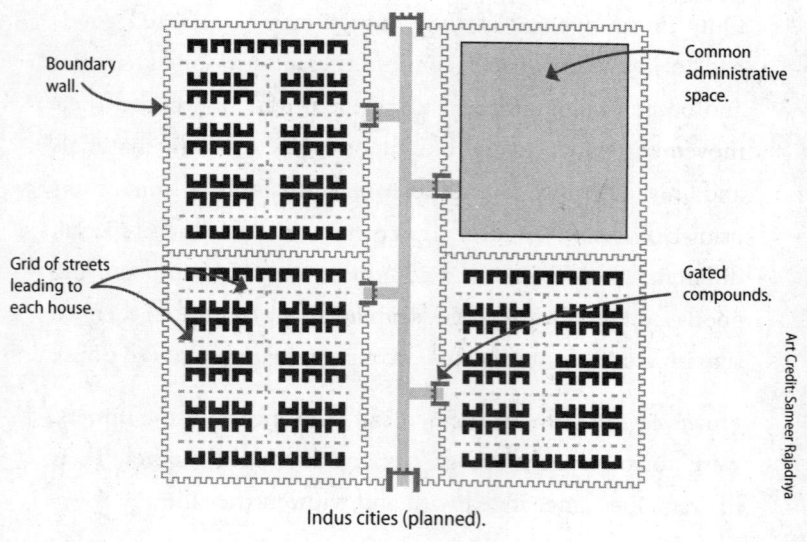

Indus cities (planned).

City plan layout.

67. Standard City Layout

To create a Harappan site, people had to follow certain urban planning rules.

▶ The site needed to be built on a platform of bricks and needed to have a wall with one narrow and carefully monitored gate for entry and one for exit. Streets had to be aligned to the cardinal directions. Doors opened inside lanes, not onto the main streets. Thus, traffic congestion was avoided. Walls were probably aligned to stars, which is why the streets are not parallel to them at many sites. Burials took place in a separate space outside the city.

▶ Cities were a collection of multiple walled communities, each with its own gate. Each walled community had homes, workshops and warehouses. Houses could be redesigned but the sanctity of the streets had to be maintained.

▶ Provisions had to be made for water (wells, tanks, rain water harvesting) and sewage disposal (drainage systems with soak-pits, sumps, traps, covers).

▶ There was one walled compound amongst others that stood distinct. Its buildings were public, administrative and ceremonial. This was the so-called citadel or acropolis, maybe the monastery of the 'unicorns'.

This was in stark contrast to Mesopotamian cities where the main streets led only to the central temple and not to individual homes. Streets were unplanned, and irregularly arranged.

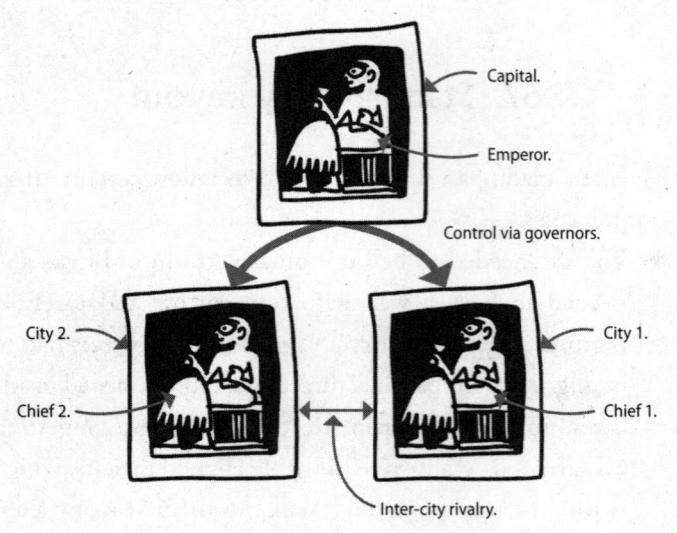

Empire and city-state model of Mesopotamia.

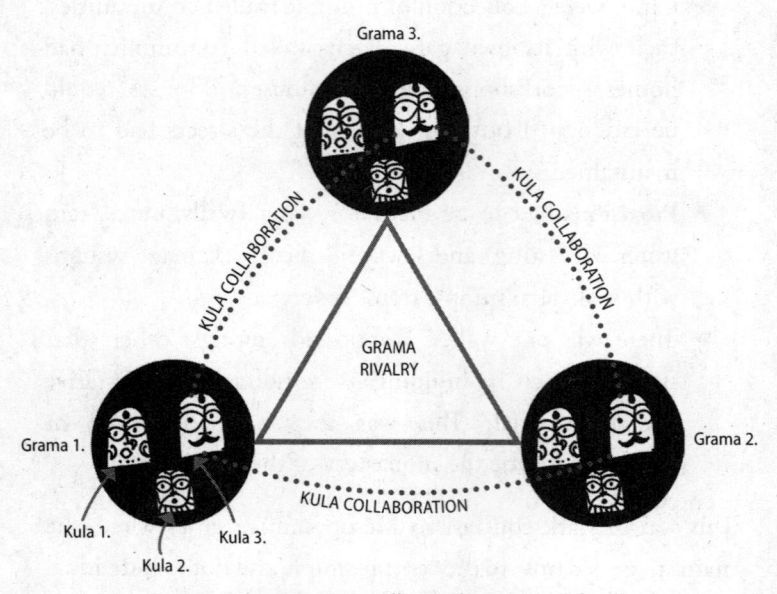

Grama-Kula system i.e., Village-Clan system of India (probably even the Greater Indus Region).

68. Heterarchy

In Harappa, it was observed that in different periods of time different gated communities prospered (improvements in buildings) or faced misfortune (neglect of buildings). This indicates absence of common concern across the city, i.e., there was no central control. They did not follow the Sumerian feudal model of city-states and empires. They probably followed a more local grama-kula (village-clan) model.

A Harappan settlement (grama) comprised many mounds. Each was a gated community (kula). These kulas competed with each other in business, but collaborated with each other to manage the entire city. A grama was a set of kulas. Each kula was spread across many gramas. This system, known as 'heterarchy', existed in later times in mercantile cities like Genoa and Venice in Italy.

The highest compound belonged to no kula. It belonged to the grama and had public buildings and ceremonial spaces. This was perhaps managed by a commonly held trust, to which every kula paid taxes. This fund was used for common activities like management of the city walls, and the city water and drainage system. Management of the 'citadel' shifted to different families sequentially. This system is found in the multiple 'mathas' of Udupi.

Great bath of the 'citadel' of Mohenjo-daro.

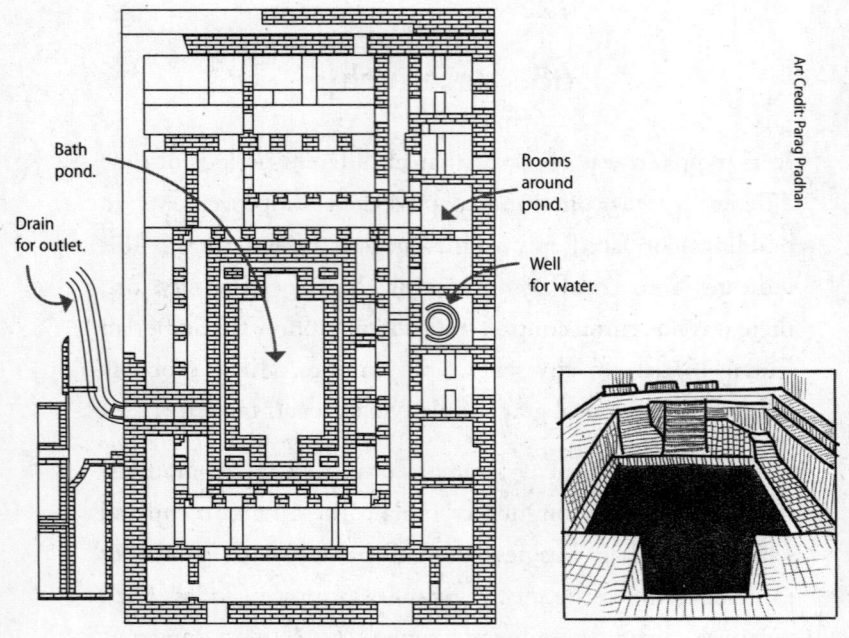

Great bath of Mohenjo-daro.

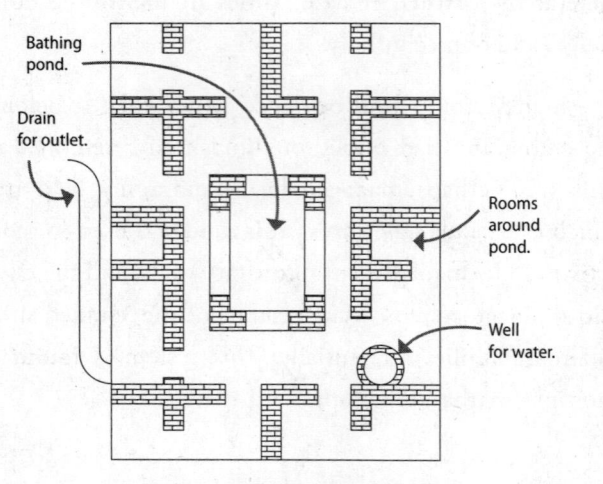

Little Bath in the 'lower town' of Mohenjo-daro.

172   *Ahimsa*

69. Modular Mindset

Harappans were modular. So most houses had the same design with courtyards leading to living rooms, work rooms, wash rooms and cooking areas. Big or small, everyone had access to water and drainage systems. Everyone had privacy. Everyone cooked in the northeast part of the house.

Hierarchy was revealed quantitatively—bigger courtyards, more rooms. There was no different design for a palace.

Words like 'citadel' and 'acropolis' and 'block' evoke European, Greek and American cultures. But all the 'common' areas of the Harappan cities had a similar structures: walls, gates, common warehouses and administrative blocks.

The 'great' bath in the common area was for all communities but in the 'lower' town there could be a 'small' private bath for one community.

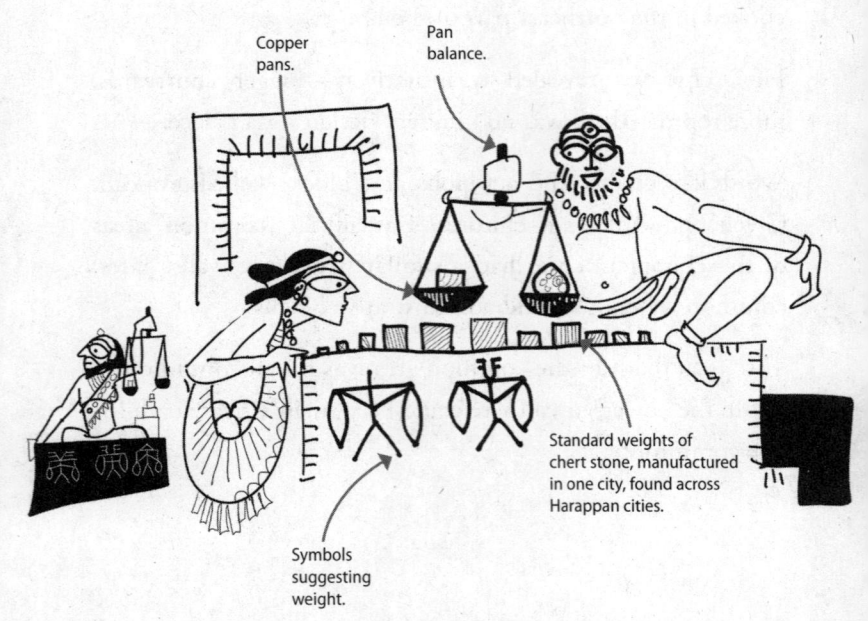

Standardized weight system of Harappa.

174   *Ahimsa*

70. Standard Measure

Different city-states of Sumer used different measuring systems, which was inefficient in trade, and indicates rivalry. In Harappan cities, everyone followed the same measuring system, thus creating homogeneity and efficiency. This common system was not imposed by any authority. It was based on nature (seeds, human body parts, leaves, reeds) and adopted by the whole culture.

- ▶ For weight, a specific plant seed (ratti/gunja) was used to create a base. It is used by goldsmiths even today. Higher weights were defined by doubling: 1, 2, 4, 8, 16, 32, 64. For higher weights, the decimal system was used: 16, 160, 1600. For these, standard chert stone weights were used across Harappan cities, perhaps made in one city—Chahnu-daro.

- ▶ For length, a body-based measuring system was used: digit, hand, span, cubit, pace. These were also used to measure the lengths and breadths of cities. They may also have used the average length of the common river reed.

- ▶ For volume, a standard was used indicated by the urn (V-shaped) symbol used with tally marks. This is found on clay tablets and on edges of pots. The V1 mark is found with 40 litre pots. The V7 with (40x7), 280 litre pots. Miniature pots, pointed goblets may have been used for smaller measures. The base unit may have been a commonly used leaf-cup or the common bottle gourd, used to make utensils.

Seals applied by bureaucrat in the common administrative block of the city, regulating movement of people, goods and services through gates.

71. Sealed Goods

Bronze Age cultures are famous for seal-based administration. Seals were used to control the movement of goods and raw material. Seals with geometric patterns, made of bone, have been identified even in early Bronze Age cultures from before 3000 BC in sites across Mesopotamia, Iran, Balochistan, Oxus and the Greater Indus Region.

Older seals have been found in graves, even graves of women of the Helmand culture of Iran. But Harappan seals are found only near gates and warehouses, indicating they were not personal, but part of a regulating system.

Seals in Sumer were typically cylindrical, made of many materials, and highly individualistic. By contrast, seals in Harappa were mostly square shaped, small (2-3 cm wide) made of white steatite, with an icon and inscription on one side and a knob with a hole on the other. This indicates the important role of institutions, and the regulation of seals.

Nearly 2,000 seals have been found till date, 80 per cent of which are from the Indus river ecosystem (Sindh and Punjab) and 20 per cent from the Saraswati river system and the Gujarat coast.

Used and old seals were broken and buried so that they could not be stolen.

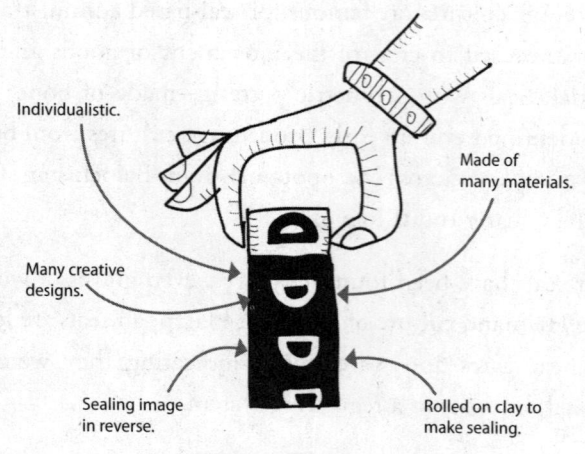

Cylinder seal of Sumer.

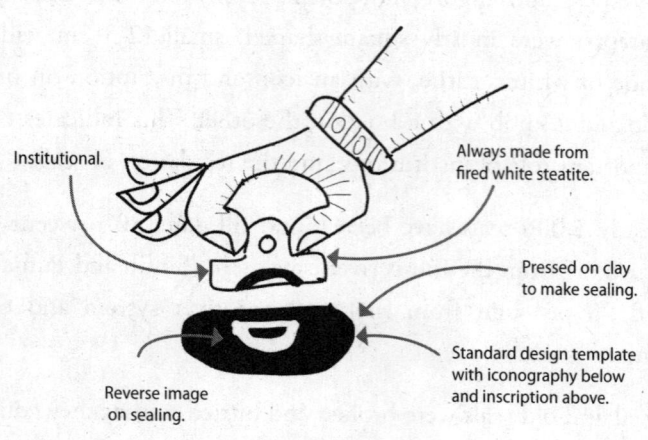

- Individualistic.
- Made of many materials.
- Many creative designs.
- Sealing image in reverse.
- Rolled on clay to make sealing.

Stamp seal of Harappa.

- Institutional.
- Always made from fired white steatite.
- Pressed on clay to make sealing.
- Standard design template with iconography below and inscription above.
- Reverse image on sealing.

72. Stamp of Regulation

In Mesopotamia, there are hundreds of seals of many materials, many styles, highly individualistic designs, indicating high diversity and low regulation. But Harappan seals were institutional, regulated and controlled—same size, same shape, same material, same design, same script.

The purpose of the seal was to regulate trade—at least the sea-trade connected with Sumer via Oman (Magan). The seals had a knob with a hole. A string was passed through the holes of many such seals and hung at gates of the Harappan cities and the many gated communities within, and stamped on clay seals or tokens. They indicated:

- ▶ License: permission to move a material or produce a product.
- ▶ Tax: what had to be paid to the city or the system that maintained the supply-chain, and how.
- ▶ Coupon: signifying who needed to be paid for services and how much.
- ▶ Challan: document confirming exit or entry of goods.
- ▶ Bill: request for payment, including mode of payment.
- ▶ Receipts: confirmation of payment, including mode of receipt.

These are financial documents. They typically have a fixed design as in stamps and license or registration documents. Everyone in the trade could understand what they meant, like road signs today. Literacy was not needed.

Finger to indicate relative size of seals and tablets.

Mythological iconography.

Twist to avoid replication.

Inscription.

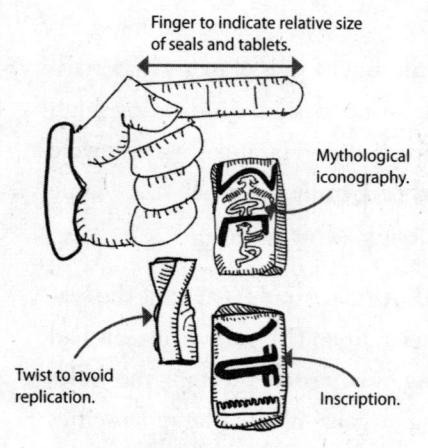

Twisted terracotta tablet from Ganweriwala, Cholistan (for ritual).

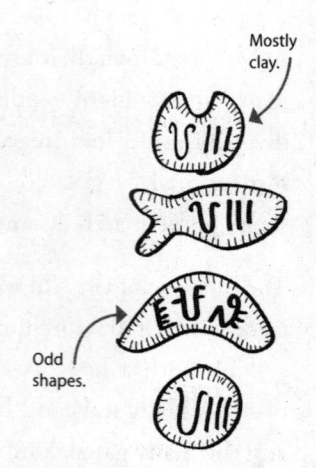

Mostly clay.

Odd shapes.

Tokens, coupons (for commerce).

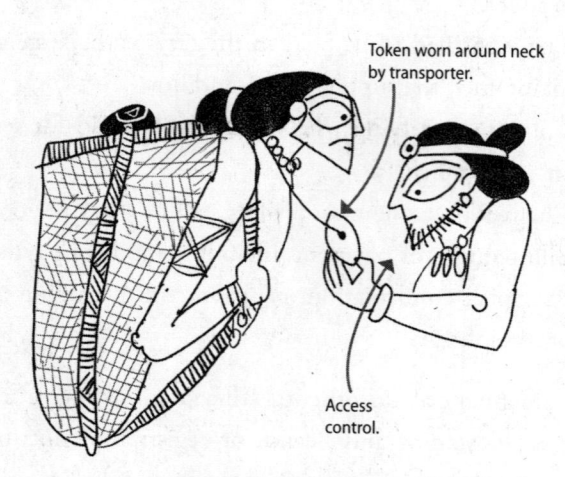

Token worn around neck by transporter.

Access control.

Token worn around neck from Kanmer, Gujarat (for access and ration).

73. Sealings, Tokens, Tablets

Seals were used to make impressions on clay sealings that would secure doors, bags, baskets, pots. When sealed objects were opened, the impressed seals were collected carefully and stored for accounting purposes. Thus seals had two uses:
- Ensuring the integrity of material during transport.
- Regulating movement that enabled licensing and taxation.

Seals were also used to create clay tokens and clay tablets.
- Tokens of many shapes (circular, triangular, oval, fish-shaped, kidney-shaped) were used as coupons or receipts, to enable distribution of rations and collection of taxes. They sometimes were perforated and worn like amulets, perhaps to identify workers who were allowed to enter certain gates and who were entitled to certain rations.
- Thin, long clay tablets with two to four surfaces usually depicting mythological imagery along with inscriptions were also used. These were often twisted. The original seal was broken. All this indicates they were created for specific events or rituals and could not be replicated. They may have been indicators of some initiation ritual or rite of passage.

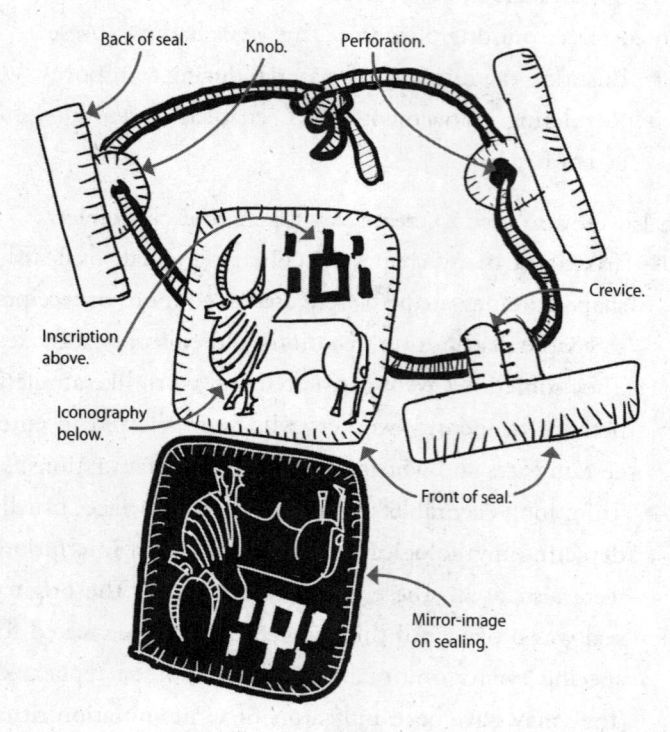

Many seals on a string.

74. Design of Seals

Most seals were carved by specialists, spread across cities, as revealed by differences in style when creating the same motif.

Seals were made using copper or bronze tools, mostly on a special soft stone called steatite, obtained from the Hazara region, which when fired turned hard and white. A few are seals made of other material including copper and silver.

Most are square-shaped, but later they became rectangular. Most have icons and inscription on one side, with a knob on the other, but some later seals have only inscriptions, no iconography, marking a new social order.

Originally seals had only geometrical patterns. These were not discontinued. But during the standardized urban phase of Harappa, we find a 'typical' design:

- ▶ Inscriptions on top, carved right to left, but read left to right on sealings. Number of symbols increase over time.
- ▶ Iconography at the bottom. A single animal, mostly male, usually facing left, with an object in front. With time, one sees the rise of mythic motifs: a fantastic beast, a sphinx, a deity with horns. The iconography disappears in the late urban phase and only inscriptions are used then, before they disappear too.

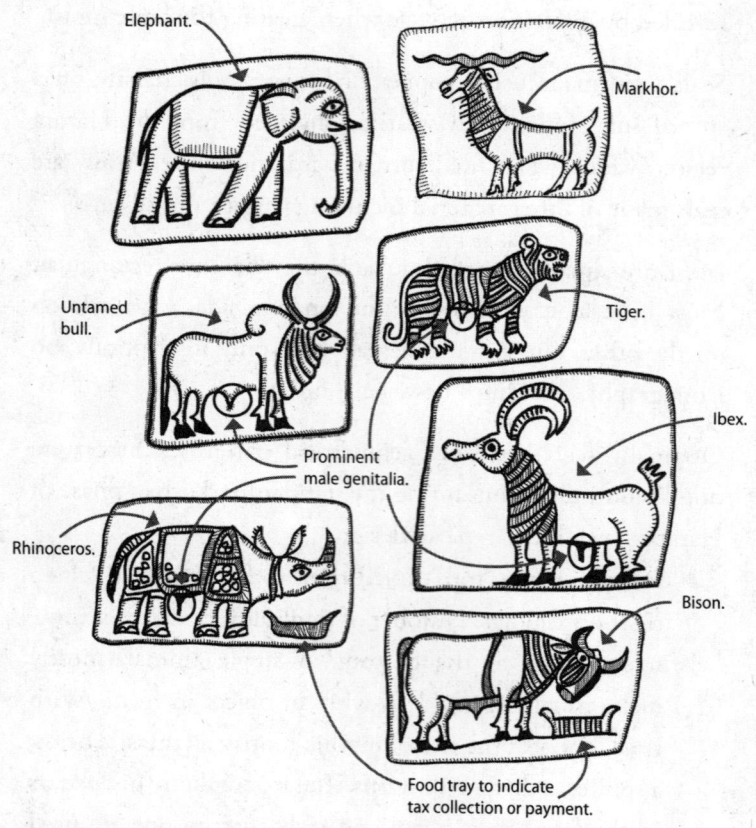

Clan symbols (all wild or undomesticated animals) that appear on seals.

75. Autonomous Clan Beasts

The iconography on seals shows a single animal. This animal is wild. If not wild, it is male (genitals always prominent), uncastrated, and so untamable and answerable to no one. The animals include: tiger, elephant, rhinoceros, wild mountain goat or antelope (difficult to differentiate), wild markhor, bison or gaur, buffalo (uncastrated) or humped zebu bull (uncastrated). Other wild animals are crocodile and hare, but these are rare, maybe of newly emerging clans.

The insistence on undomesticated animals indicates power and autonomy. These were probably clan (kula) symbols, marking a guild that lived in a gated community, and had relations through marriage with other similar gated communities with the same clan animal.

- ▶ Sometimes, the tiger or the elephant would have a horned headdress, indicating greater superiority.
- ▶ Sometimes even the wild animal would be shown with its head lowered, eating from a food tray. The food tray probably indicated tax claimed. Even in the eighteenth century Maratha empire, licenses and taxes were referred to as 'food portion' that one is entitled to, and documents were signed with the phrase 'Eat what is yours'.
- ▶ No tray is ever seen before the naturally horned zebu bull. Does it mean independence from food, outgrowing hunger, a movement towards the monastic ideal, like the unicorn that prefers 'perfume dispenser' to 'food tray'?

Ring of beasts (many clans).

Tigers (same clan, many cities).

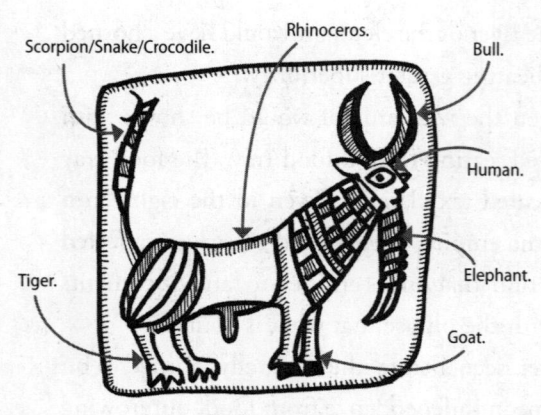

Scorpion/Snake/Crocodile. Rhinoceros. Bull. Human. Elephant. Tiger. Goat.

Composite beast (many clans).

Collaborative symbols.

186   *Ahimsa*

76. Collaborative Mythical Beasts

Wild animals are highly territorial. Clans are highly competitive. To reduce conflict, the Harappans would have developed toolkits of collaboration. Usually this was done through marriage or dining together. But what if clans maintained caste-like purity, using a contemporary 'roti-beti' custom that creates 'jati', whereby a clan does not share bread (roti) or daughter (beti) with others?

In that case, collaboration would be achieved by a common deity, one who is above hunger and so does not seek food (share of market), like Durga born by amalgamating Vedic gods, or village-goddess festivals where every constituent clan performs one ritual.

This is indicated by images of mythical animals, which always involve clan animals and a unicorn, or 'horned' priest.

▶ There is a ring showing heads of many animals: bison, bull and unicorn.
▶ There is a common three-headed beast: bison, goat/antelope and unicorn.
▶ There is a creature that seems to be an amalgamation of all wild creatures: tiger hindlegs, goat/antelope forelegs, a rhinoceros underbelly, a unicorn neck, an elephant head, bull/buffalo horns, even a human face.
▶ Even the animals in the 'pashu-pati' image are all clan animals: crocodile tail, tiger, buffalo, rhinoceros, elephant, and goat/antelope.

Face upwards as if sniffing air.

Script.

Incense burner.

Unicorn seal.

Clay figurines of unicorns found at many sites prove that the unicorn is not a misinterpreted two-dimensional image of urus or auroch.

Ahimsa

77. Unicorn Image

Nearly 80 per cent of Harappan seals have the image of the unicorn. These appeared and disappeared with the rise and fall of Harappan standardization. So those who used this seal clearly enabled the 'veneer'. These could be administrators. The mythical symbol was perhaps an animal that all clans agreed upon. Or the one-horned creature had special meaning, indicating other-worldliness and so fairness, ideas that we encounter in later times, after 200 BC.

- ▶ Chinese court chronicles from the Han period refer to a cow-like unicorn that came from a distant land and could identify and impale guilty people in the court of justice.
- ▶ The Buddhist Jataka and Hindu Mahabharata, tell the tale of a one-horned Rishya-shringa, born when a hermit mated with a female deer. As long as he was innocent of women, he had magical powers to stop rain. When he was seduced by women, the drought ended, and rains returned.

Twenty of 500 signs are used 50 per cent of the time.

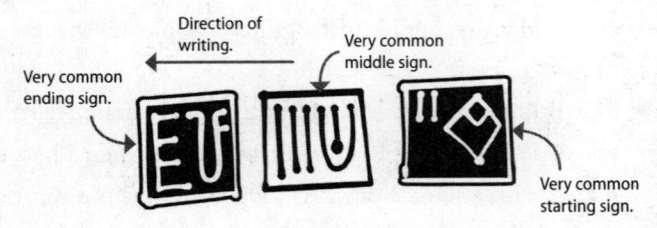

Pattern of writing as revealed by statistics.

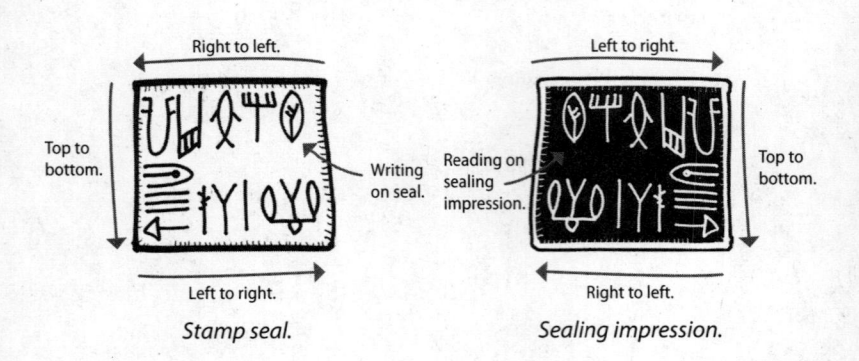

Stamp seal.

Sealing impression.

78. Script

Most Harappan seals have an inscription above the animal iconography. Sometimes the inscription is found without the iconography, either on seals themselves, or inscribed on the neck of pots, amulets, copper plates, inside shell and stoneware bangles, even on bronze blades. This inscription is clearly a script.

Its origins lie in marks once made on pots by potters to serve as 'brand' markers identifying the maker. But a script is more evolved.

- There are roughly 400-600 unique symbols, of which around fifty are used more frequently than others.
- They are used in short inscriptions, a set of five to twenty symbols.
- Older seals show fewer inscriptions.
- The symbols were carved right to left on seals, then top to bottom, then left to right. On sealings, the mirror image could be read in reverse: left to right, then top to bottom, then right to left.
- Statistical analysis shows the symbols are not randomly placed. They follow a clear pattern (grammar?) with frequently used start and end symbols.
- Symbols are used in mercantile contexts (warehouses, gatehouses, pots, tokens, coupons) and religious contexts (ritual clay tablets) but never seen in graves.
- The pattern changes in Oman, indicating that the same symbols could be used to express different ideas.

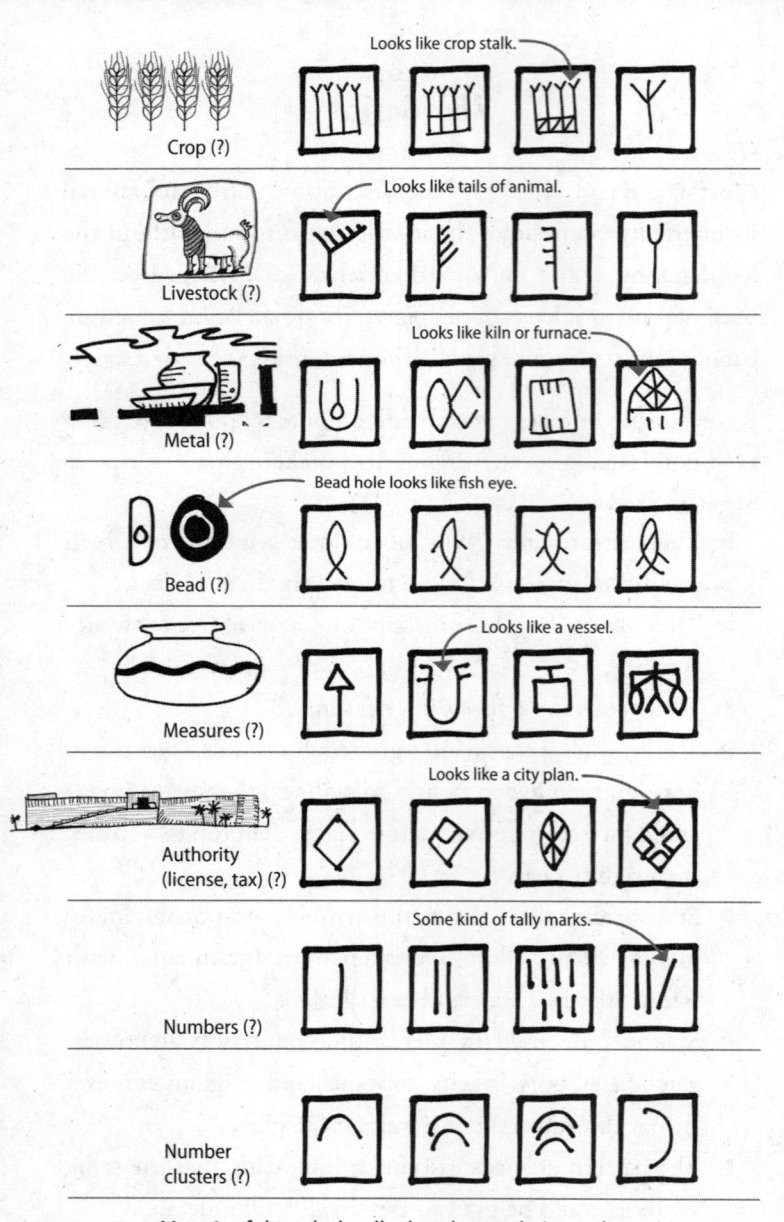

Meaningful symbols, all related to trade (speculation).

79. Meaning or Sounds

Writing was invented by accountants who used images originally to indicate commodity and numbers, for the purpose of record-keeping. The Harappan script communicated meanings, not sounds. So they were like mathematical notations and emojis, not like alphabets. They were used primarily to indicate financial transaction. There were symbols indicating:

- ▶ Raw materials (plant, animal, mineral, metal, dye).
- ▶ Finished goods (beads, fabric).
- ▶ Services (transport by cart, boat, humans).
- ▶ Authority (city, enclosure, route).
- ▶ Measurement system (weight, volume, length).
- ▶ Numbers.

These can be guessed based on the images. For example, an arrow-shaped line indicates a reed that may have been standard measurement for length, or a jar with or without rims was used to measure certain volumes; crops were indicated using images of the stalks, animals by images of the tail. Mesopotamians refer to fish-eyed beads so the fish symbol probably referred to beads. Ivory was referred to using symbols of the elephant. Different coloured birds perhaps referred to different dyes.

Tray in front (domestication).

Wild animal.

Uncastrated hence untamed bull.

No tray in front (sovereignty).

Untamed bull.

Ibex looking back (special status).

Unicorn looking up (independence).

Bison looking down (submission).

Composite three-headed beast.

Symbolic language.

80. Symbolic Language

Harappans clearly understood symbolic language. This is evident in inscriptions and iconographies.

- All animals used are wild, symbolizing independence. Always the ibex or markhor, never the domestic goat.
- All animals used are conspicuously male, symbolizing resistance to domestication. No sign of the holy cow of Vedic times.
- The use of horns to indicate power, worn by men, women, mythical beings, both those giving and receiving offerings, as well as wild animals.
- The repeated presence of plants in the background indicates either wilderness or fertility.
- Directions clearly have meaning: walls and streets are aligned in cardinal directions. Animals face left or right or turn around. This clearly indicated some form of conformity, defiance and middle path.
- Wild animals eating from a 'domestic' food tray indicates some form of control.
- The absence of food trays before the mighty zebu bull may indicate self-reliance.
- The 'unicorn' is never shown eating from a tray below but sniffing a perfume from a typical incense burner, turning its head upwards, towards the sky not the earth. Does this mean transcending earthly concerns—grace rather than gravity?

- Concave neck.
- Used for cooking lentils and pulses.
- Convex body.

Harappan Handi.

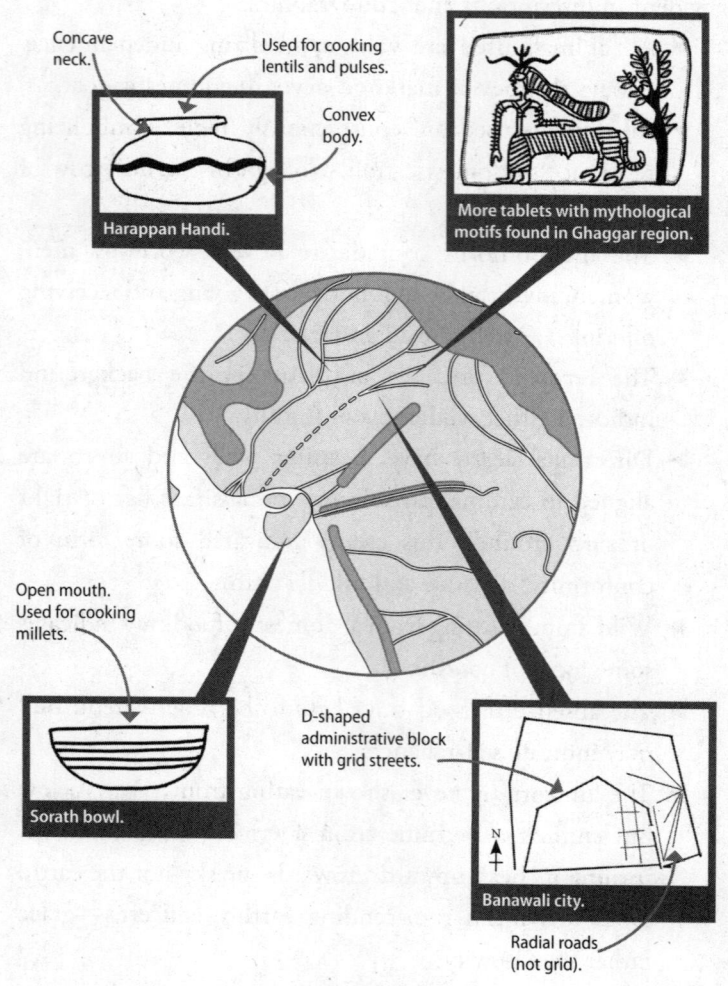

More tablets with mythological motifs found in Ghaggar region.

- Open mouth. Used for cooking millets.

Sorath bowl.

- D-shaped administrative block with grid streets.

Banawali city.

- Radial roads (not grid).

Map showing diversity.

196   Ahimsa

81. Diversity under Veneer

Harappan homogeneity was a veneer. It was spread across cities separated by distances of 500 to 1,000 km. There was an underlying diversity.

- While unicorn seals make up 80 per cent of seals, it is only 25 per cent in Banawali (Haryana). More mythological-themed imagery is found in Kalibangan (Rajasthan).
- Most Harappan seals have icons of animals facing left. But there are a significant few (especially in the Ghaggar river basin) that face right.
- Gujarat sites use a lot of stone rather than brick for building houses.
- Gujarat sites show preference for millets and therefore cup-shaped utensils, over wheat and handi-type utensils found in other sites.
- People in different parts of the land spoke different languages and so the script had to be 'meaning-based' rather than 'sound-based', like the mathematical symbols (+, -, %, >) we use today.
- Only a fraction of the people were buried. Others would have cremated the dead, exposed them to the elements, cast them into the river, or fed them to animals and birds.
- The use of old geometrical seals made of bone and terracotta continued despite the appearance and domination of white steatite square seals with knobs behind.

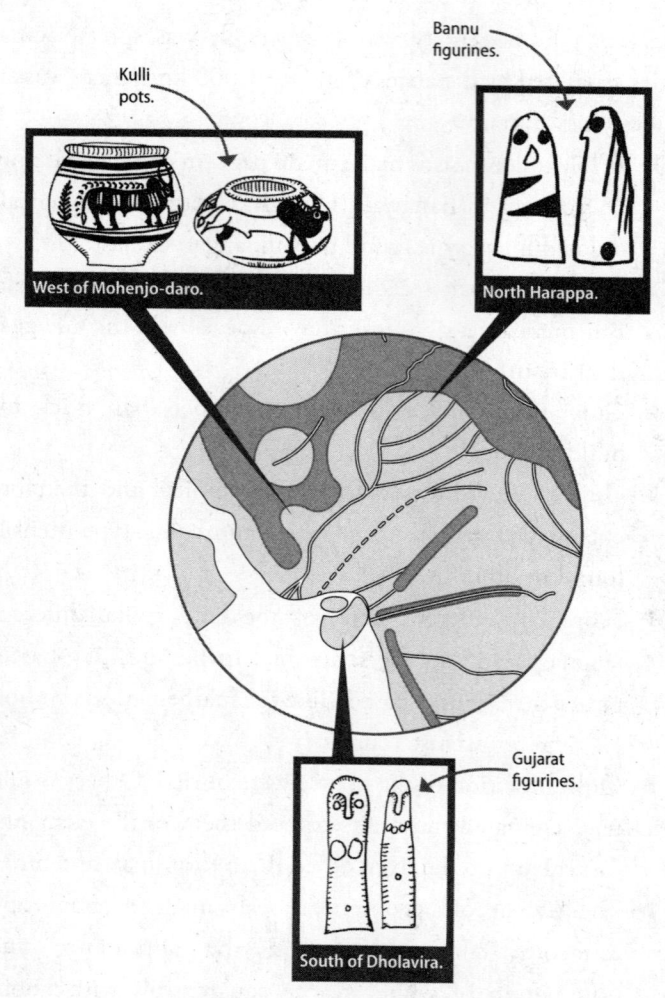

Absence of standardization.

82. Resisting the Veneer

Many parts of the Greater Indus Region did not participate in this integration process.

- ▶ North of Harappa, despite availability of rich fertile lands north of the Ravi river, there are very few Harappan sites.
- ▶ The old site of Kot Diji on the east bank of River Indus was burnt, and overshadowed by Mohenjo-daro. One is not sure if this fire was deliberate or accidental or an act of violence.
- ▶ The old site of Mehrgarh, near Bolan Pass in the Kacchi plain, which had its own character, was overshadowed around 2500 BC by the site at Nausaro, which was Harappan. Movement through the pass was restricted until after 2000 BC. Kulli culture to the west of Bolan Pass was distinct but with some shared features (dish on stand, perforated vessel, zebu bull art, female figurines).
- ▶ There are more Harappan sites in the northern part of Gujarat. In the southern part (Sorath), millet was grown and the region had its own type of pottery with handles, different from the standard black on red ware of Harappa.
- ▶ Finger-like female figurines in Gujarat are curiously similar to figurines in the northern Indus region (Bannu culture).

Mehrgarh figurines, pre-Harappan, from near Bolan Pass (3000 BC).

People

Culture is eventually about people: their cravings and insecurities. Bound by rules of credit and debit, Harappans did not hoard. They shunned conflict, resisted new ideas, feeling safe within walls, gates and courtyards, with their seals. Clan rivalries festered—with status demonstrated using beads and bangles. Not everything was about economics (artha) and politics (dharma) though. There was the pleasure (kama) of spicy food, of colourful clothes, maybe song and dance, even if consumption meant more debt—a warning given by sages meditating under the peepul tree.

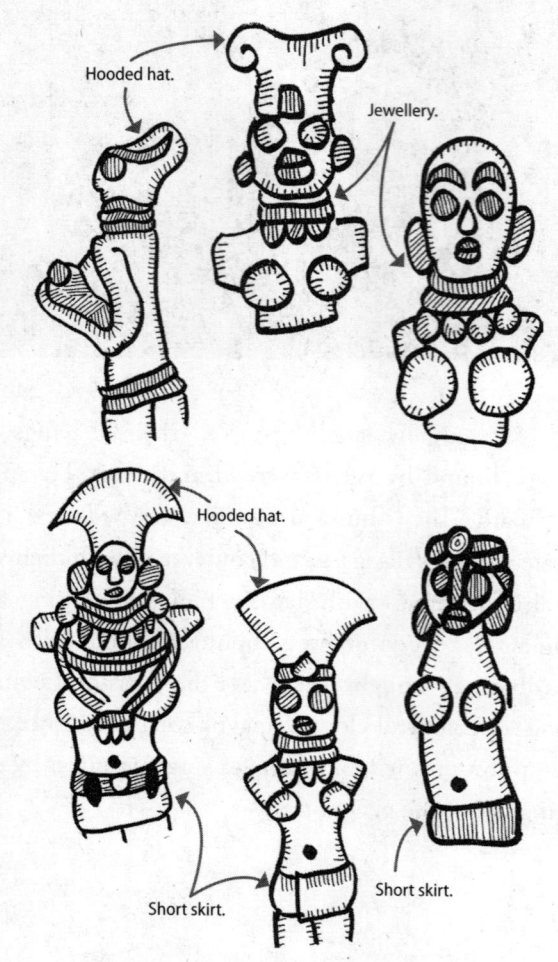

Harappan female figurines (2000 BC).

83. Mothers or Goddesses

In the cities of Harappa and Mohenjo-daro, many clay figurines of bejewelled women have been found. The images are rather crude, perhaps part of a domestic ritual ceremony, like the present-day vrata. Most clay images are female, in direct contrast to the virile male animals found on seals.

The head and trunk is amplified more than hands and feet. But you get a sense of how the women adorned themselves. The women have elaborate headdresses, beaded chokers and necklaces, bangles, beaded girdles. Was this fashion or ritualistic, like 'shringar' of Hinduism—meant to be auspicious and attract good luck and fortune? In Harappan graves, copper mirrors were found with women only.

The earliest such images have been found in Mehrgarh. There too the women have elaborate hairstyles and headdresses, accentuated breasts, feet together. Emphasis on a woman's role in reproduction using jewellery (attracting the male) and enhanced breasts (nourishing the child) does suggest importance placed on fertility in an age of high maternal and infant mortality rates.

Apart from being mother figures, could these also be goddesses? In the Helmand basin of Afghanistan-Iran, burial sites reveal women with button seals, designs of which are different from button seals buried with men. They clearly had roles related to the manufacture of goods, beyond domestic responsibilities.

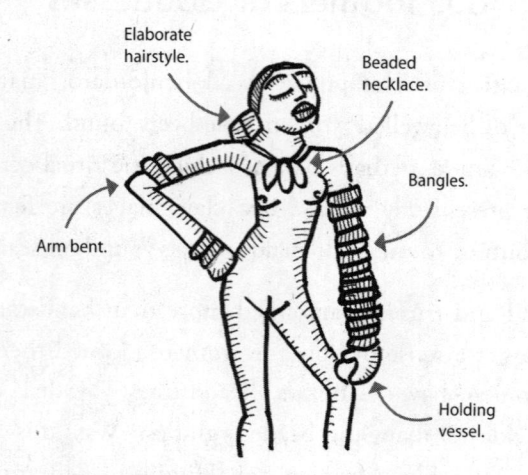

Dancing girl of Mohenjo-daro.

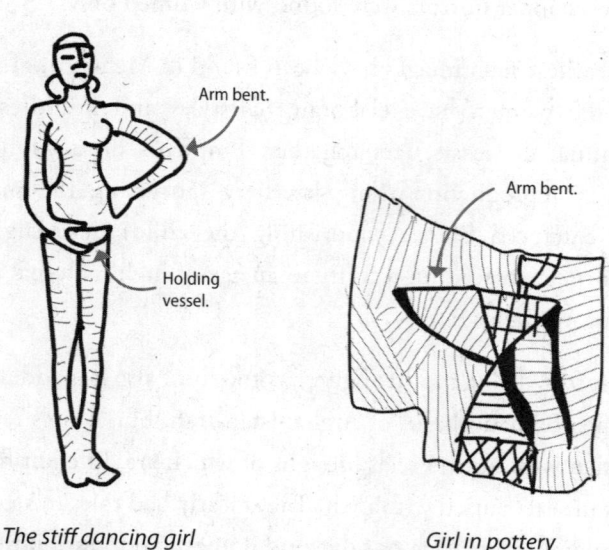

The stiff dancing girl (Karachi Museum).

Girl in pottery (Bhirrana, Haryana).

Ahimsa

84. Why a Dancer

A 10 cm tall bronze statue of a young girl made using the lost wax technique was found in Mohenjo-daro. She wears no clothes, but has many bangles around her left arm, a few around the right, three beads around her neck, an elaborate hairstyle, and a confident stance.

Her stance reminded British archaeologists of nautch girls they had encountered in India, so they described her as a 'dancing-girl' though there is nothing about her posture that suggests dance. This is how the male gaze, the colonial male gaze, works. The name has stuck.

Her features seem Afrocentric and so her roots could be the First Indians, the earliest migrants into India 50,000 years ago from Africa. It must be kept in mind that the Rakhigarhi skeleton's DNA indicated a connection with India's tribal population.

A second figure, now in Karachi, was also discovered in Mohenjo-daro, but is of inferior craftsmanship, does not have the same relaxed pose, but does have one arm is folded at the hip. The same stance is seen in a potsherd recovered from Birhanna. Clearly there is a deeper meaning to the woman's stance that escapes us. The other hand holds a vessel—is it an offering for a deity, food for her family, or food for herself?

206   *Ahimsa*

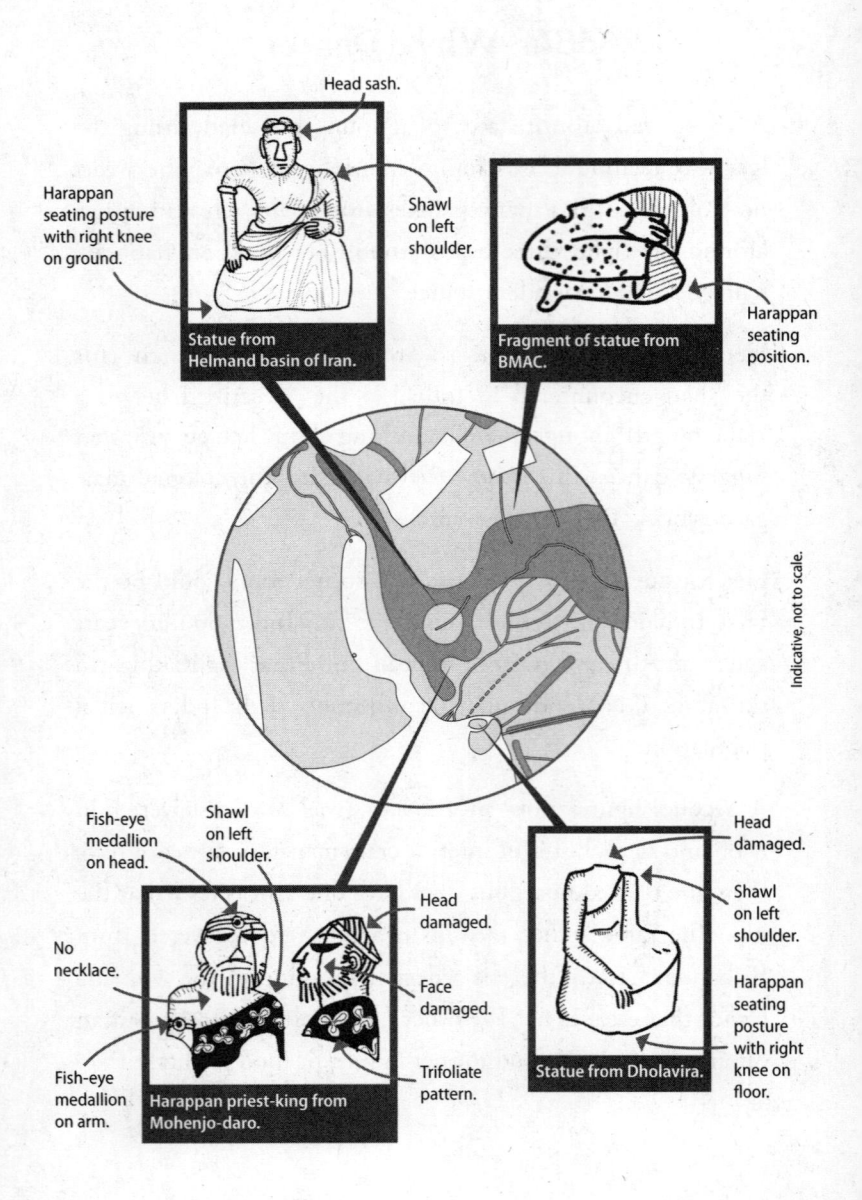

85. Not a King or Priest

A 17 cm tall steatite image of a bearded man, with no moustache, half-closed eyes, and a shawl over his left shoulder, was found in Mohenjo-daro. He has a round medallion tied to his forehead and his arm, revealing the fish-eye inlay motif. The shawl has a trifoliate pattern. It was probably painted with a blue-green base and red flower patterns, like the palash (flame of the forest) tree. The hollow socket had inlay eyes. It is conventionally identified as 'priest-king'.

We do not have the lower half of his image, but a 65 cm tall headless bust of a man with a shawl on his left shoulder has been found in Dholavira. He sits in the typical Harappan posture: with left knee up and right knee on the ground. Similar images of a head and of a headless torso have been found in Helmand culture. They look similar to bearded images found in Oxus culture. All these images come from the final phase of Harappan cities, and seem to have been vandalized.

Was this a foreign ruler? Why is the same image found in these faraway places that were important trade routes? That the 'priest-king' appears around the time that 'falcon' seals from Oxus appear indicates a shift in balance of power, a waning of old Harappan systems.

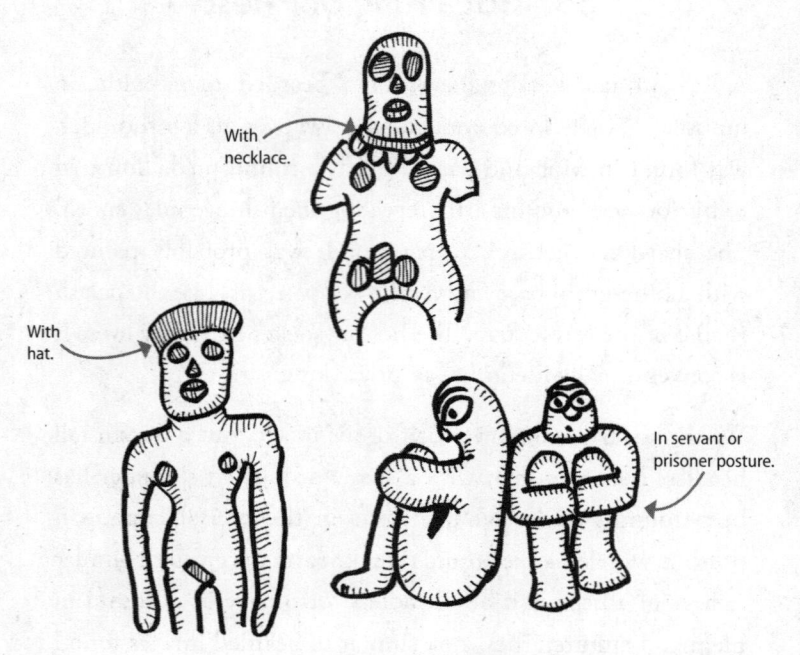

Male images on terracotta.

Male images on clay tablets.

208   *Ahimsa*

86. Men

A few terracotta statues of men have been found. They are shown with prominent nipples and genitalia. There are images of men seated in a crouching position like prisoners. Were they slaves? There are images of men with a conical cap. Were they the masters?

More information about male imagery comes from seals and tablets. The men are shown wearing few clothes, maybe a loin cloth. Bangles are used to tie their hair too, suggesting men kept long hair. The hair is tied in a double bun with a sash. People in ritual acts seem to wear a horned headdress. Men wore bangles, anklets and beaded necklaces but were generally less bejewelled than women. There are images, and a crude statue, of men with spears attacking bulls. Men are seen making votive offerings to deities emerging from trees.

The stone statues of authoritative bearded men, with shawls draped over their left shoulders, could be of foreign origin as they are found in later layers. Conventionally they have been described as 'priest-king', but that seems rather presumptuous.

The presence of predominantly female terracotta images and predominantly male wild animals in seals suggests a clear gender differentiation in society.

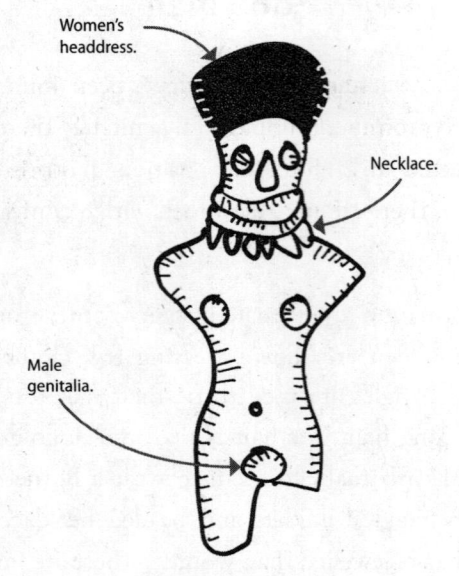

Queer figurine(?).

Androgynous horned sage.

87. Queer Folk

There are terracotta images found in Harappa with prominent male genitalia but jewellery and headdresses typically linked to women. Were these androgynous or queer people? We must not impose our gender norms on ancient societies.

Harappan imagery does not show a strong male or female orientation. There is no overt display of genitalia in the seals. The headgear of the deity is partly male (horns) and partly female (a flowing sash like the Chitral kupa or the Tibetan perak). The 'deity' also wears bangles, and so one wonders if the deity emerging from the tree, or seated in a meditative stance, is male, female, both or neither.

What looks like an erect phallus in seal art to some looks like a girdle to others. The seven dancers with plaits could be male or female cross-dressers. Cross-dressing is an important part of many rituals.

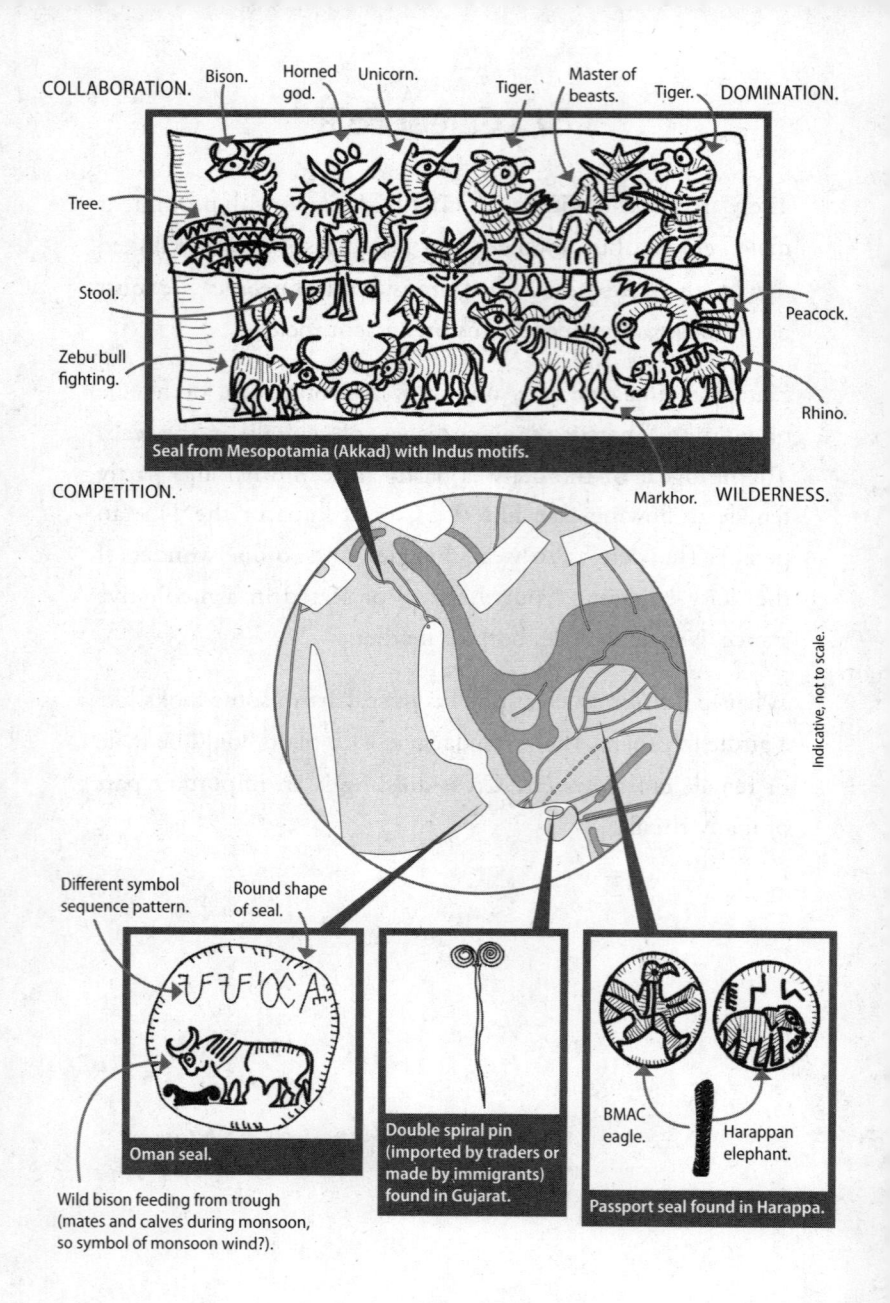

COLLABORATION. Bison. Horned Unicorn. Tiger. Master of Tiger. DOMINATION.
god. beasts.

Tree.

Stool.

Peacock.

Zebu bull
fighting.

Rhino.

Seal from Mesopotamia (Akkad) with Indus motifs.

COMPETITION. Markhor. WILDERNESS.

Indicative, not to scale.

Different symbol
sequence pattern.

Round shape
of seal.

Oman seal.

Double spiral pin
(imported by traders or
made by immigrants)
found in Gujarat.

BMAC
eagle.

Harappan
elephant.

Passport seal found in Harappa.

Wild bison feeding from trough
(mates and calves during monsoon,
so symbol of monsoon wind?).

212   *Ahimsa*

88. Migrants

As a trading community, the Harappan civilization was remarkably insular. Goods such as seals and carnelian beads from the Greater Indus Region are found across Mesopotamia but goods from Mesopotamia are not found in the Greater Indus Region.

There are clear indicators that merchants and craftsmen may have migrated to Mesopotamia via Oman and established a 'Meluhhan' village. This is evident in pottery styles found at sites, as well as artwork created with local materials but with Harappan techniques and motifs. So there are Mesopotamian cylinders that have unique Harappan motifs: the humped bull, the horned deity, the peacock.

But there seems to be some indication of inward movement of people from Central Asia via the Bolan Pass towards the latter part of the Harappan urban period.

- ▶ Tablets with an elephant on one side and a falcon on the other.
- ▶ The double-sided pin in parts of the Greater Indus Region, at Chanhu-daro (Sindh), Mehrgarh (Balochistan), Burzahom and Manda (Kashmir), Banawali (Haryana), Kuntasi and Rojdi (Gujarat).
- ▶ The image of the so-called priest-king who kneels on one knee, which is also found in Oxus and Helmand cultures, besides Mohenjo-daro and Dholavira.

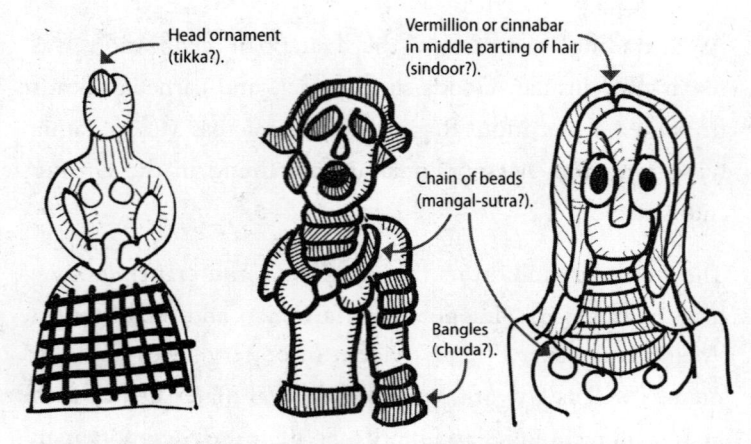

Symbols of marriage as revealed by figurines from Harappa and Mehrgarh.

Matrilocality.

89. Marriage

Harappan seals and tablets do not show images of couples or families. There are images of wild animals, animal hunting and domestication, offerings made to deities, women separating fighting men, men wooing tigers or leaping over bulls, but nothing linked to romance or eroticism.

That both men and women enjoyed wearing bright clothes and elaborate jewellery is the only indicator of sensuality. The women took copper mirrors and bangles to their graves; the men took beaded necklaces with them.

A study of bones in burial grounds show that women were closely related. This indicates matrilocality. Women stayed with their parents and did not move to their husbands' houses, at least in the urban areas. This is common in many mercantile communities of coastal India like Kerala and Mangalore, where the daughter stays at home, and her husband—the sailor—comes and goes with the monsoon. Maybe the mercantile Harappans followed this practice, with husbands travelling between cities, and women staying with their parents. This changed with the arrival of Aryan men, who preferred wives staying with them. Stories of wives leaving their husbands and returning to their parents' home is a common theme in early Vedic literature (stories of Urvashi and Saranya), indicating Harappan women took time shifting to new marriage arrangements.

Farmers and herders may have had different practices.

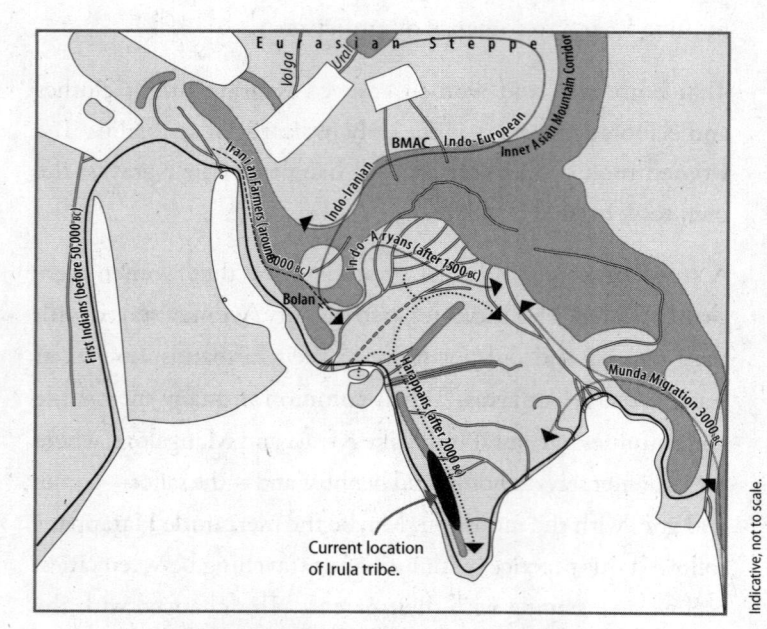

Migration of peoples into and around India.

90. Genetics

Europeans were obsessed with 'race' in the nineteenth century. They saw Sumerians as a mysterious dark-skinned race from the east (Dravidians?) that were overwhelmed by the Akkadians who were of Semitic origin. They argued that Harappan cities were built by Dravidians and destroyed by fair-skinned Aryan invaders who came from the north. None of these ideas make sense as per DNA analysis, which clarifies the following:

- Humans entered India along the coast from Africa over 50,000 years ago.
- Nomads from Iran came via the Bolan Pass to India around 10,000 years ago.
- Harappans spread along the Ganga river basin and to southern lands along the coast 4,000 years ago, when cities ceased to function. Some may have spoken proto-Dravidian languges.
- The Aryan gene entered India 3,500 years ago.
- Endogamy (marrying within caste) began 2,000 years ago.

The DNA from the single female found in Rakhigarhi is similar to the DNA of the Irula tribal folk, who live far away in Tamil Nadu. This means the Greater Indus Region was populated by local people. They traded with foreign lands but there were no foreign invaders or rulers.

The Irula tribe is famous for catching snakes and rats, and collecting honey. They worship a goddess and her six sisters who created the first man and woman.

Harappan deity.

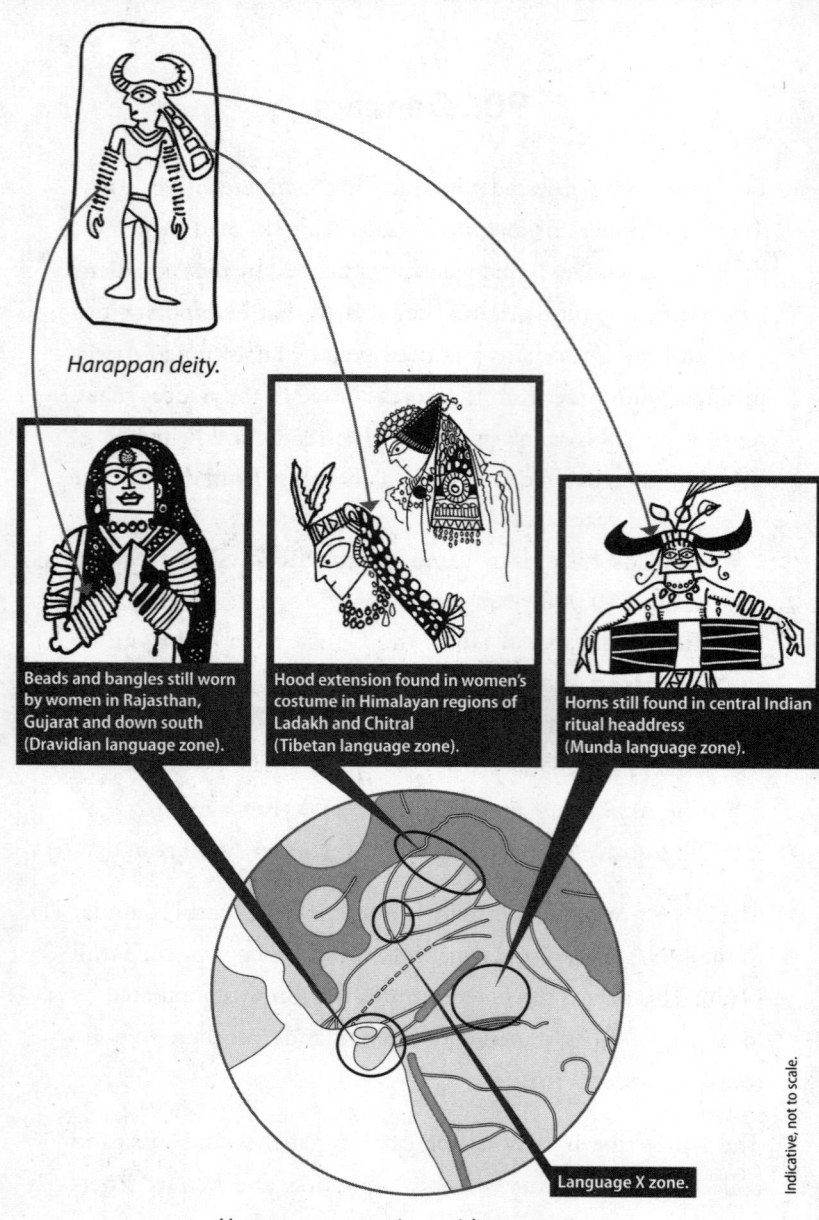

Beads and bangles still worn by women in Rajasthan, Gujarat and down south (Dravidian language zone).

Hood extension found in women's costume in Himalayan regions of Ladakh and Chitral (Tibetan language zone).

Horns still found in central Indian ritual headdress (Munda language zone).

Language X zone.

Indicative, not to scale.

Harappan connections with current times.

218   *Ahimsa*

91. Language

The people of Harappa spoke many languages.
- In the northern part they may have spoken the Tibetan language. The hooded headdress of women in Ladakh and the Chitral province of Pakistan is found on Harappan seals.
- In the central part they may have spoken a para-Munda language. The horned headdress continues to be seen in the Mariah tribe of central India, where the Munda language is spoken. Munda migration happened from Southeast Asia nearly 5,000 years ago and they introduced wet-rice farming.
- In the southern part they may have spoken a proto-Dravidian language. Even today the Brahui language of pastoral folk in Balochistan is a Dravidian isolate. Words for sesame and ivory found in ancient Mesopotamia are derived from proto-Dravidian words. Some of the oldest Tamil poetry retains a memory of the migration from the north: memories of yak, bone-eating camels, wild donkeys in salt pans.
- The retroflex sound is unique to South Asian languages and is found in the Vedas but not in the Iranian Avesta. This was introduced by Harappan mothers. This sound is found amongst Australian aborigines, and so belonged to the First Indians who migrated out of Africa 50,000 years ago.
- Hindi has egrativity grammar, which probably came from Harappan languages.

Pottery showing story of clever crow.

Pottery showing story of cunning fox.

220   *Ahimsa*

92. Stories

Harappan pottery art reveals some stories that Harappans told each other:

- ▶ A deer is unable to drink water from a pot but a crow is able to do so by putting pebbles in the pot, causing the water level to rise. This is a story of using creativity to solve problems.
- ▶ A fox gets a bird to drop the meat in its beak by praising its voice and encouraging it to sing. This is a story of trickery, warning against flattery.

Merchants across the world, in later times, saw India as the home of stories. Stories from India such as the Panchatantra and the Ramayana made their way to Europe, Arabia and Southeast Asia. Clearly, teaching valuable lessons through parables was already part of the Harappan mercantile network.

Youth playing pithu or lagori.

Mechant playing a board game with dice.

Farmers doing bull leaping.

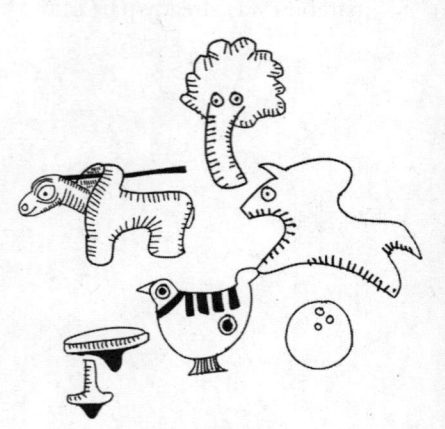

Toys for children.

Ahimsa

93. Games, Sports and Pastimes

Children in Harappa played with terracotta toys: miniature figures of sheep, goats, tigers, bulls, buffaloes, rhinoceros, even dogs, partridges, pigeons. Many of these toys were mobile—with wheels and moving mechanical necks.

A set of terracotta cakes of gradually decreasing size indicates the children played the game 'pitthu' or 'lagori'.

The presence of dice and pawns indicates the presence of board games such as the famous 'board game of Ur'.

Rooster fighting was probably invented in the Harappan cities, from where it spread to Sumer. Ram fights, bull fights, goat fights were common public events. Bull leaping was a sport too, played in ceremonial grounds.

For a people who lived in segregated communities, within courtyards, entertainment was a release. Much of the games were played indoors with occasional outdoor events during pubic ceremonies.

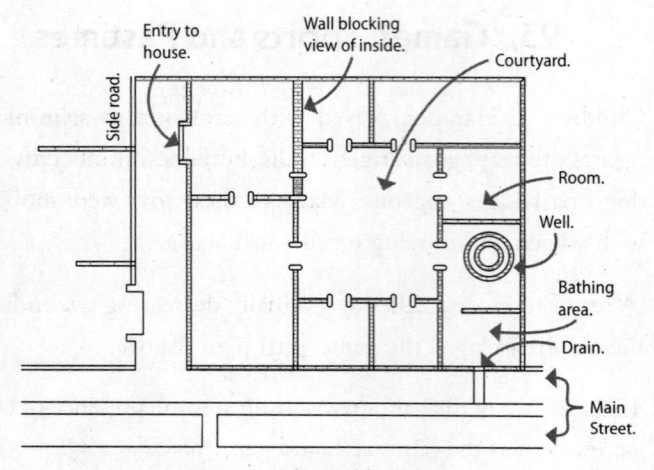

Harappan home blueprint.

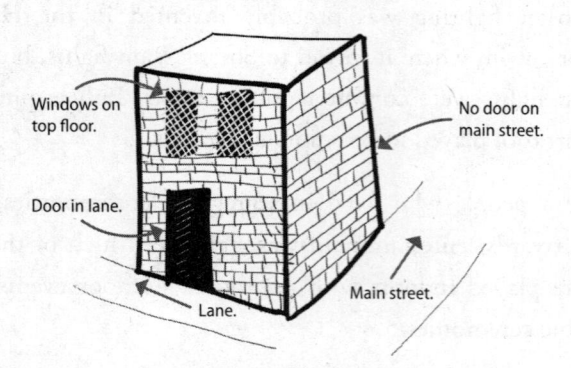

Front view of house.

Reed house outside cities.

94. Homes

The Harappans' urban homes show a preference for privacy.
- ▶ They were located in a gated compound.
- ▶ Houses were on brick platforms, with elite houses located higher than others.
- ▶ Doors did not open on the main street. They opened on side lanes.
- ▶ The main door faced a wall so that no one from the street could see the inside of the house.
- ▶ The houses mostly had a courtyard that was surrounded by many rooms.
- ▶ Most houses had one or two floors, for which there were wooden stairs.
- ▶ Windows opened towards the courtyard on the ground floor but outside from upper floors.
- ▶ The houses had wooden doors and windows, and reed mats.
- ▶ The floor had patterned tiles similar to pottery designs.
- ▶ Every house had a bathing platform and a latrine.
- ▶ Elite houses had private wells but most had common wells.
- ▶ There were small single-room houses that were meant for servants.

Farmers probably lived in reed houses. There are reed houses shown in many clay tablets that are remarkably similar to reed houses found in Southern Iran, located amongst palm trees.

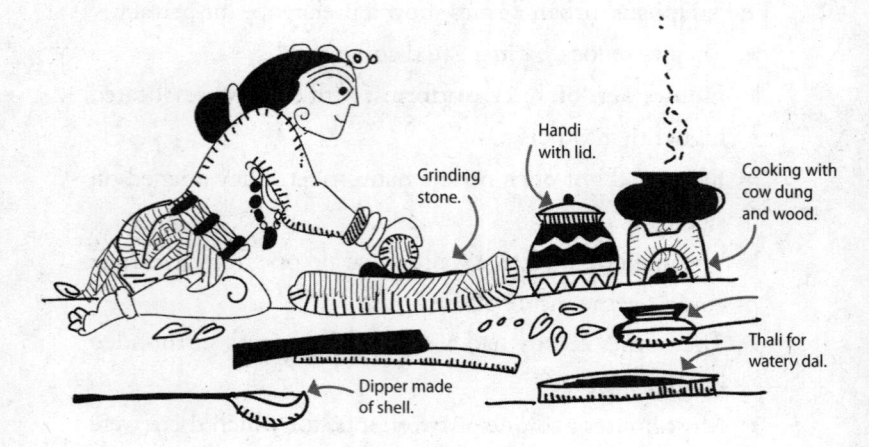

Harappan kitchen.

Perforated pot always found within larger pot (for lautering process of beer making? for cheese making?).

95. Kitchen

The Harappan kitchen was mostly located in the north-eastern corner of the courtyard, which received sunlight first. This eventually became the most sacred corner of the Hindu household.

Cooking involved use of firewood and dung fuel.

The kitchen had grinding stones to make flour and masala. They had a range of cooking vessels including the traditional Indian cooking pot: the handi, which has a relatively narrow mouth with a neck and rim and a rounded base, that allows for heat to be retained in the lower part and stay relatively cool in the upper part. This allows for slow-cooking of pulses and lentils.

The Harappans probably ate on plates and cups of leaves, which is a common Indian practice. There may have been utensils of wood and cups made of pumpkin gourd. Terracotta lotas (small rimmed pots) and pointed goblets were used to consume liquid. A copper thali suggests the Harappans ate watery food like dal, as Indians do today.

Millets were probably cooked as porridge and ragi are cooked today, in wide-mouthed cups like the ones that have been found in Gujarat, where millet is grown.

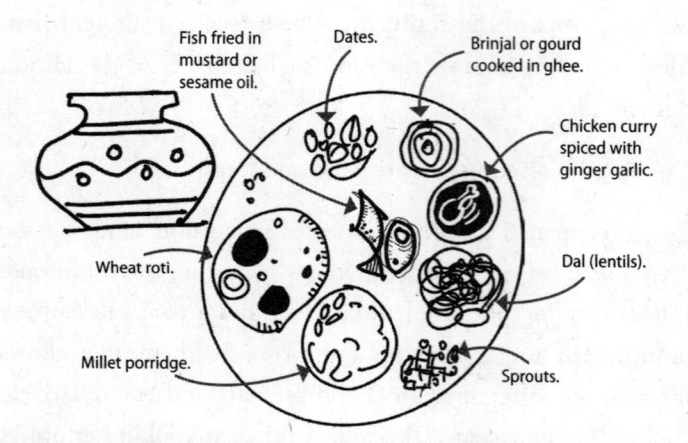

Harappan thali: was food presented in a circular format as it is today?

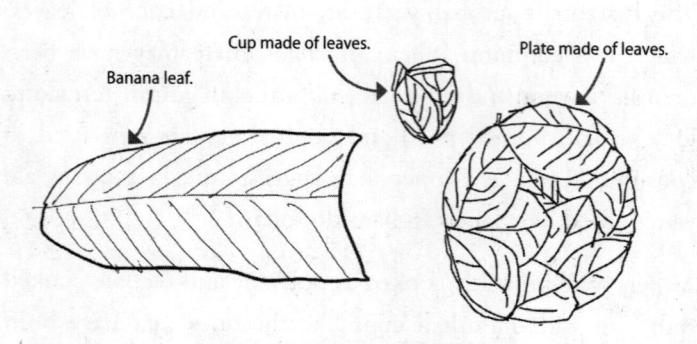

Leafy plates may have been used.

96. Food

The Harappans invented masala, cooked in oil, ate dairy products, meat, fish and a host of cereals, pulses, legumes, vegetables and fruits.

- ▶ Vegetables: brinjal, gourds, radishes, moringa, cucumber.
- ▶ Green vegetables: spinach (palak), fenugeek (methi).
- ▶ Cereals: wheat, barley, millet (jowar, bajra, ragi), probably rice.
- ▶ Pulses: pigeon pea (tur), chickpea (chana), green gram (mung), black gram (urad).
- ▶ Fish: saltwater and freshwater.
- ▶ Meat: chicken, mutton, beef, buff, pork, wild game. Cattle were kept in homes, fed millets. Goats moved with nomadic people.
- ▶ Dairy: curds (lactose intolerance was widespread until Aryans arrived) and ghee.
- ▶ Fruits: jujubes, melons, grapes, dates, probably mango, sugarcane, tamarind.
- ▶ Oil: sesame, mustard.
- ▶ Spices: onion, garlic, ginger, turmeric, coriander, cumin, fenugreek, probably pepper.

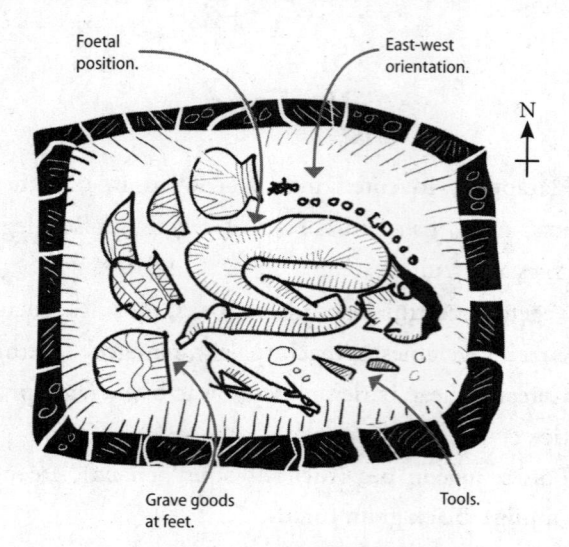

Pre-urban phase grave.

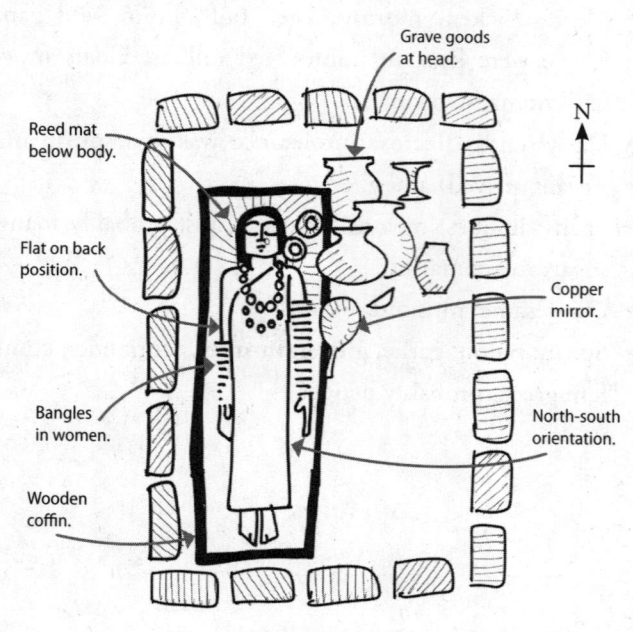

Urban phase grave.

97. Burials

The Harappan civilization was made of many communities each with a different burial practice. This is why we have disproportionately few burial sites, compared to the large population that lived in the cities. We are talking about thirty generations of 20-40,000 people, and barely a few hundred grave sites.

Burial, when practiced, involved placing the body in a wooden coffin, on the back, head to the north, in a grave lined with bricks, oriented in the north-south direction. The grave typically had a fixed ratio: 1:1:2, once again revealing the Harappan obsession with proportions.

Women were typically buried with their left arm covered with bangles. And they were buried with copper mirrors. Clearly shringar or ritual adornment of women was part of Harappan culture.

Men had fewer bangles. Bangles were also used to tie their hair in some cases. Men also had strings of tiny steatite beads. A few beads were of gold, others of semi-precious stones and some were made of clay.

MEMORIAL
(SIDE VIEW).

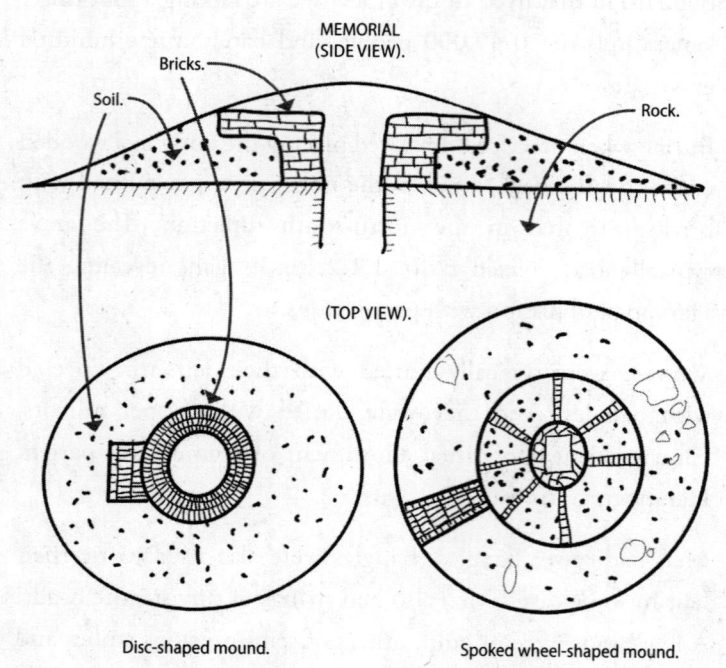

Soil. Bricks. Rock.

(TOP VIEW).

Disc-shaped mound. Spoked wheel-shaped mound.

Grave in Dholavira with no skeletons.

98. Memorials

In early societies, humans buried their kith and kin under their houses or their agricultural lands. In Harappan cities, the dead were always taken outside the city, either exposed to the elements or buried in specially designated areas. Before and after the Harappan 'veneer' existed, bodies that were buried were always on their side, curled in a foetal position, with pots towards the feet. However, during the urban period, the body was typically flat on the back, with the head as well as pots to the north.

The Gujarat region has revealed many Harappan sites with a necropolis (city of dead), i.e., a section of the city with a vast number of graves. These are either rock-cut graves, or pits lined with stones (cist), with a mound of rocks (cairn) above them, or a circular brick platform around them, resembling either a spoked wheel or a solid wheel.

What is most remarkable is that many of the graves in Dholavira have no bodies. They are symbolic. The bodies were disposed of in other ways. Or perhaps these are memorials built to remember, or honour, those who died at sea during a trading mission to Magan. Travelling over 1,000 kilometres on a reed boat was surely not easy, without sails, without knowledge of the stars or the monsoons. Or could these be connected with the mound burials (kurgan) of Eurasian steppes?

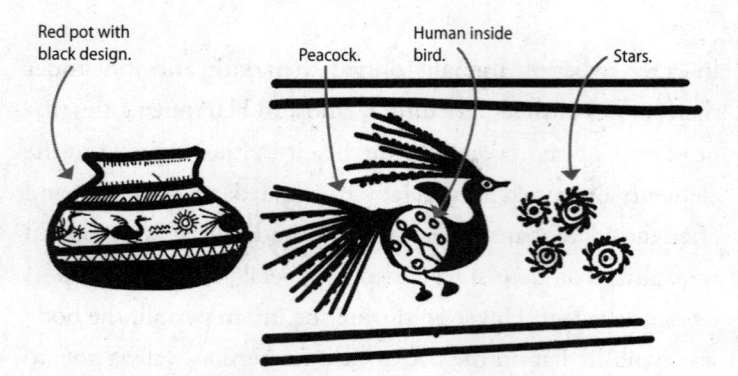

Burial pot from Cemetery H (Punjab) dated 1900 BC to 1300 BC.

Burial pots from Gandhara (north of Harappa city) that looks like a human face, dated 1200 BC to 800 BC.

234   *Ahimsa*

99. Pot Burials

After 1900 BC, when the Harappan cities ceased to exist, burial patterns changed dramatically in the Sapta-Sindhu region of Punjab. First, the bodies buried stopped being aligned north-south and started being aligned east-west. Instead of being placed on the back, the bodies returned to the old foetal position, seen in old burial sites.

More and more pot burials happened, mostly containing the bones of people who had either been cremated or exposed to the elements. The pots were red with black designs of peacocks, with humans within them, travelling towards the stars.

Further north of the Indus river basin, in Swat valley that later came to be known as Gandhara, there were grey pots containing ashes of people who had been cremated, as well as clay figurines, never seen in Harappan pots. The pots sometimes resembled human faces.

The rising popularity of cremation and pot burials signalled a change in mythology, a new way of looking at life and death.

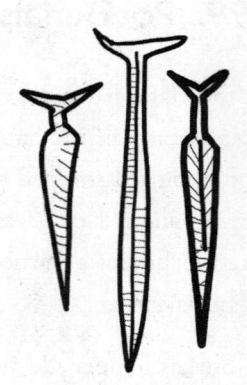

Antennae swords.

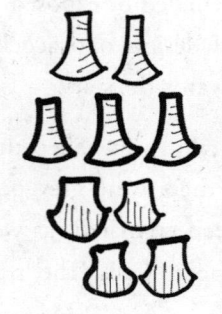

Axe heads.

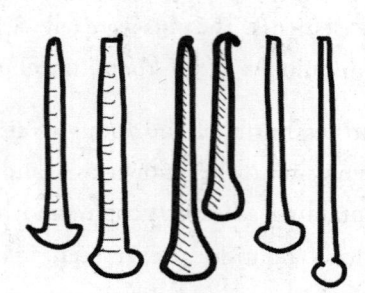

Clubs.

Harpoons.

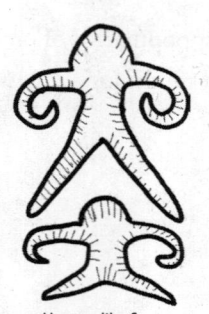

Human-like figures.

*Copper hoards found in
Ganga-Yamuna river basin (1700 BC to 1200 BC).*

100. Hoarding Copper

During the Bronze Age, everyone in the Greater Indus Region sought copper and tin. Bronze was precious. But at the end of the Bronze Era, from 2000 BC to 1500 BC, we find communities to the east, in the Ganga river basin, burying large hordes of copper weapons in ritual ceremonies. Was this a symbolic rejection of copper, as the Iron Age dawned? Communities figured out how to create a high temperature (1500 degrees Celsius) that enabled them to make iron tools from easily available iron ore. The locus of culture was also shifting away from River Indus towards River Ganga. The people perhaps remembered stories of the Saraswati river disappearing into the desert.

The Mahabharata was written in Sanskrit around 100 BC and it tells stories from the Vedic period, 1000 BC. It speaks of the Pandava warriors, who lived near the Yamuna and Ganga, hiding their weapons in the forest. Could these be memories of the copper hoards? We can only speculate.

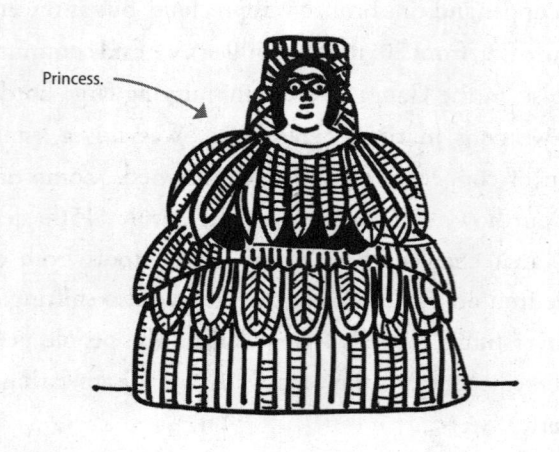

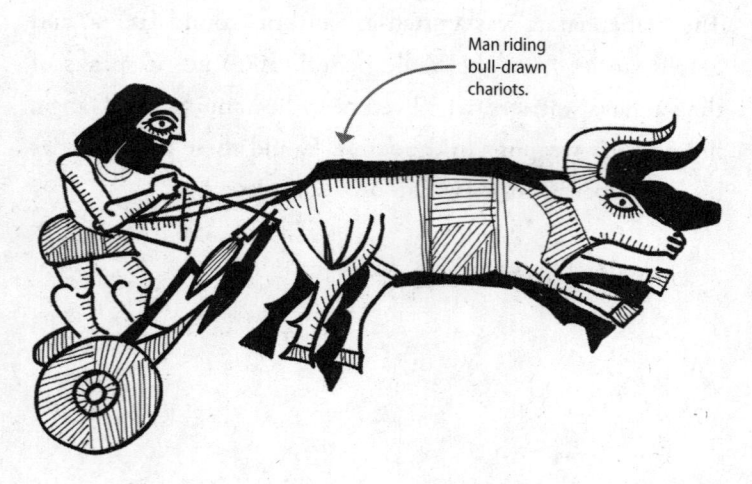

Artifacts from BMAC.

CONCLUSION
(Post) Harappan Mothers and Aryan Fathers

Many Hindus of the twenty-first century are spellbound by the Vedas, especially as understood through the Ramayana and Mahabharata. When we locate them in a timeline, we realize the following:

- Harappan cities traded 4,000 years ago.
- Vedic rituals were performed 3,000 years ago.
- The Ramayana and Mahabharata were finally put down in writing 2,000 years ago.

Verses from the Ramayana and Mahabharata are used to explain the origins of Indian history, bypassing all that archaeology reveals.

But science does not care for politics. It does not care for Brahmins or the British. It just presents facts.

Facts can be used in many ways. For example, fire pits at the Kalibangan site can be ovens to the secular eye, and sacrificial altars to the religious eye. What is a 'dock' in Lothal to Indian archaeologists appears like a 'tank' to other archaeologists. We can use facts to argue about what we want our past to be. Or we can use it simply to expand our understanding of humanity. Take the case of snakes and eagles.

- ▶ Snakes and eagles are conspicuous by their absence in Harappan art.
- ▶ Eagles and snakes are common themes in artworks found in Mesopotamia, BMAC, Helmand, Elam, Jiroft. These are cultures that Harappans traded with. These are all located west of the Hindu Kush.

The final phase of the Harappan cities (1900 BC) saw seals from Central Asia. These had the image of raptors.

The following is one story from Sumerian mythology, as narrated in ancient cuneiform tablets dated to 2000 BC, about the rivalry between eagles and snakes. Eagles and snakes were once friends, until the eagle ate the serpent's babies. Enraged, the serpent bit the eagle repeatedly, striking its wings until it was no longer able to fly. A king, Etana, saved the eagle from certain death. In exchange, the eagle promised to take the king to the heavens to obtain a herb that would give him a great son. But as the bird rose higher and higher, Etana became dizzy and fell to the ground.

Jiroft art from Southern Iran showing eagles.

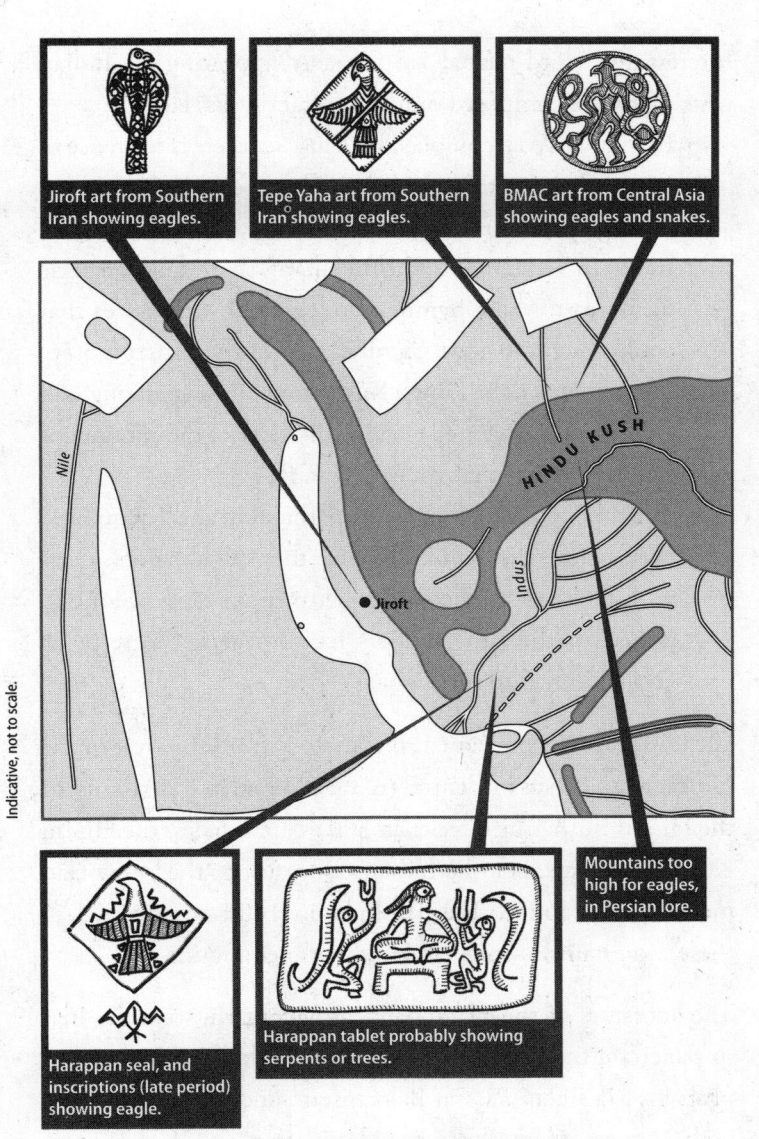

Tepe Yaha art from Southern Iran showing eagles.

BMAC art from Central Asia showing eagles and snakes.

Mountains too high for eagles, in Persian lore.

Harappan seal, and inscriptions (late period) showing eagle.

Harappan tablet probably showing serpents or trees.

Indicative, not to scale.

Eagle-serpent motifs in cultures to the west and the east of the Hindu Kush.

Conclusion

241

Interestingly, bird-related stories start appearing in Indian texts that were composed only a thousand years later.

- ▶ In the Rig Veda, compiled by 1000 BC, there is reference to Manu, the ancestor of Indian Aryans, receiving Soma from the eagle from far above the mountains, which he offers to Indra. In Vedic rituals, the fire-altar is shaped like an eagle facing east. Vedic hymns were equated with eagles that could reach the gods. Significantly, in the contemporary Iranian Avesta, the Hindu Kush mountains separating Iran from India are referred to as 'upari-saena' or the 'mountains that rise higher than an eagle can fly'.
- ▶ The earliest Vedic epic, Suparna-akhyana, composed even before the Ramayana and the Mahabharata, deals with the story of the rivalry between an eagle (Garuda), linked to the sun, and his half-brothers, the serpents (Naga) linked to the night.

Clearly, there is a movement of the story from the west of the Hindu Kush (Oxus in Central Asia, Helmand in Iran) to east of the Hindu Kush. The Greeks, in 300 BC, referred to the Hindu Kush as Indukus, i.e., the Indian Caucasus, or the 'snow-clad mountains of India'. The Muslims, in 1000 AD, referred to these mountains as 'killer of Hindu armies and slaves'.

The ancestors of the Harappans, at Mehrgarh, were the first to penetrate this mountain range even before 7000 BC, most probably via Bolan Pass in Balochistan, and establish contact with cultures on the western side, in Iran and Afghanistan. This enabled them to obtain rare lapis lazuli, and tin, for themselves first, and then for the world markets. This supply chain played a crucial role in the rise of Harappan cities.

Later, times changed. Those on the western side of the mountains found direct routes to Mesopotamia and West Asia. Harappan cities declined.

But then a new technology rose in Eurasia, lands far north of the Himalayas.
- ▶ By 2200 BC, horses were domesticated north of the Caspian Sea in the steppe grassland near the Don-Volga river basins.
- ▶ By 2000 BC, spoked-wheel war chariots were invented that were light enough for these horses to pull. Grave sites at Sinthasta near the Ural river basin of Southern Russia show these chariots and horse bones.

Demand for this lethal military technology made the horse-breeders from the Eurasian Steppes migrate westwards and eastwards.

The westward arm moved towards Greece, Asia Minor, West Asia, Egypt and Mesopotamia. The eastward arm settled in BMAC for a time, where they got used to thermogenic and energizing drink of ephedra, made from a leafless shrub that grows high atop the mountains, known as:
- ▶ Homa in Persian.
- ▶ Soma in Sanskrit.
- ▶ Huo-ma ('fiery hemp'), or Hu-ma ('barbarian hemp') in Chinese.

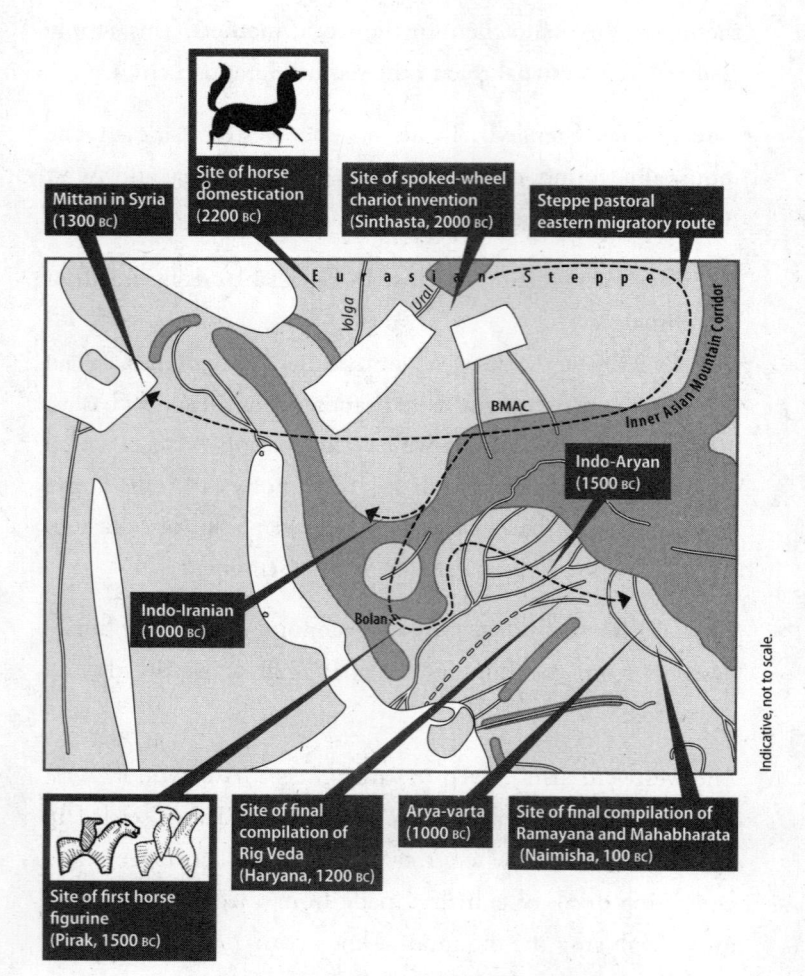

Map showing migration of steppe pastoralist men.

244   *Ahimsa*

The horse-breeders and chariot-riders who drank this drink at BMAC split into three groups around 1500 BC.

- ▶ The western arm reached Syria where Mittani clay tablets mention horses, as well as Vedic gods: Indra, Varuna, Mitra, Nasatya.
- ▶ The southern arm of Ariyas moved towards Iran, and would eventually compose the monotheistic Avesta where 'div' refers to demons.
- ▶ The eastern arm of Aryas moved towards India, and would eventually compose the polytheistic Rig Veda were 'deva' refers to gods.

Those who came to India came without wives, as revealed by DNA analysis. They married local women, whose ancestors may have built the Harappan cities. With the Aryans, the locus of culture shifted from the west of the Thar desert to the east of the Thar desert. In the Yamuna-Ganga basin one finds a flurry of activity after 1500 BC.

- ▶ Buried hordes of copper weapons, as if symbolically rejecting violence: 'antennae' swords, axe handles, arrow heads, harpoons, and human-like cult objects from 1800 BC to 1200 BC. At one burial there is even a wagon, that is assumed to be a chariot but unlikely as the wheels are solid and there are no horse bones or bits nearby.
- ▶ Shifts in pottery styles in the Ganga basin indicating migrations and mingling resulting in cultural shift:

Black on red pottery of Harappan period (2600 BC to 1900 BC)

Pots of Gandhara grave culture (1200 BC to 800 BC)

Ochre coloured pottery (OCP) with copper hoards (1500 BC-1000 BC)

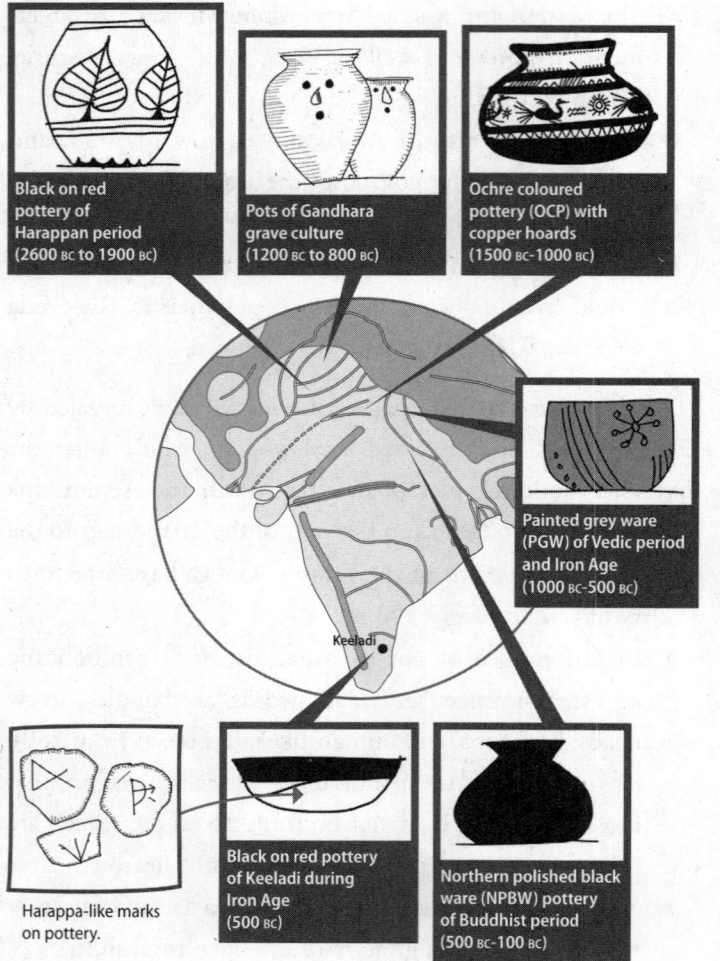

Painted grey ware (PGW) of Vedic period and Iron Age (1000 BC-500 BC)

Indicative, not to scale.

Keeladi

Harappa-like marks on pottery.

Black on red pottery of Keeladi during Iron Age (500 BC)

Northern polished black ware (NPBW) pottery of Buddhist period (500 BC-100 BC)

Map of India showing shift in pottery styles over time.

246 Ahimsa

- Ochre coloured pottery (1800 BC to 1500 BC).
- Red and black ware (1500 BC to 1000 BC), which continues without interruption in the south.
- Painted grey ware (1000 BC to 500 BC).
- Northern black polished ware (after 500 BC).

▶ Rise in iron technology after 1000 BC, that allowed for greater penetration of the thick Gangetic forests. Iron is easy to access but tough to melt, as opposed to copper that is easy to melt but tough to access.

▶ Rise in rice farming, agricultural surplus, mercantile networks, monastic orders, and finally kings seeking to put tolls on trade routes, after 500 BC.

▶ Writing of Sanskrit epic poetry, such as Ramayana and Mahabharata, after 100 BC, that recalled an ancient time (1000 BC?) when kings venerated Brahmins.

Today, 160 generations after the Harappan period, 120 generations after the Vedic period, eighty generations after the earliest Sanskrit epics, forty generations after the earliest regional translations of those Sanskrit epics, we need to remind ourselves that like the Harappans of yore, many of us still:

▶ Cook in handis, eat in thalis, and drink from lotas.
▶ Enjoy masala (ginger, garlic, turmeric) and vegetable oil (sesame, mustard).
▶ Drape ourselves in bright cotton clothes.
▶ Wear strings of colourful beads (mangal-sutra), bangles (chuda) and other rings to indicate marital status.
▶ Use the gesture of joined palms (namaste).

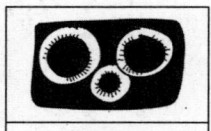

Bangles
Handi and Lota
Peepul
Sacred Bull
The Sawai flag of Jaipur indicating status of 1.25
Namaste

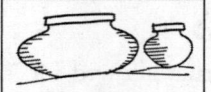

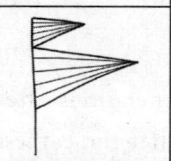

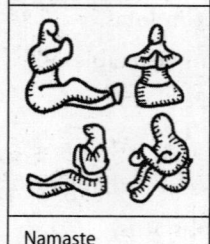

Continuity.

- Venerate cardinal directions (digga-pala).
- Divide the sky into twenty-seven lunar asterisms (nakshatra).
- Worship trees (banyan, banana, neem).
- Worship animals (bull-god Basava, buffalo-god Mhasoba, tiger-god Vaghoba, scorpion-goddess Chellamma).
- Venerate androgynous monks and mystics.
- Measure using seeds (ratti).
- Use cowries as currency.
- Count using fingers (1,2,4,8,16).
- Perform rituals using flowers, fruits, vegetables, leaves, cloth and colour powder without permanent shrines.
- Use amla, shikakai as soap and detergent.
- Use combs and pins to create elaborate hair styles.
- Believe in 'nazar' or evil eye and the protective power of stones.
- Live in houses with courtyards (aangan).
- Bathe before eating and value purity (madi).
- Enjoy symmetry in patterns (rangoli).
- Value proportion 5:4 (sava-ser, 1.25, metaphor of extraordinariness).
- Use symbols in household rituals to represent gods (dots, lines, circles, trident).

Ahimsa

Aryan man meeting (post) Harappan woman.

- Use a sacred low table for placing holy objects (pidha).
- Enjoy diversity, negotiate borders and resist attempts to impose uniformity.

In other words, in our obsession with the Vedas we are so focussed on Aryan fathers that we forget Harappan mothers. We forget that the Indian river has many more tributaries besides the Vedic one. It is not just about warriors (Kshatriyas) and their poets (Brahmins) but also about merchants (Vaishyas) and craftsmen (Shudras) and mendicants (Shramanas). Later came the Greeks, the Persians, the Scythians, the Parthians, the Huns, the Turks, the Afghans, the Arabs, the Central Asians, the Europeans. Just as Harappans resisted a central authority, just as they balanced standardization with diversity, we still resist attempts to homogenize India into a single idea. That is why India has never had one great empire, or one single god, prophet, or monk, determining its destiny.

Tigers are common on Harappan seals, but never mentioned in Rig Vedic hymns. Acacia tree, however, is seen in Harappan seals and mentioned in Rigvedic hymns.

Acknowledgements

This is not an academic book. It is meant for the general public. The aim is to simplify, not complicate, and to stir interest using known facts, and informed speculation. What we know about the Harappan civilization is the result of work done by hundreds of scholars, over a hundred years. Scholars belong to different countries, different cultures, different universities and are shaped by different myths (ideologies), like the object of their study. Their knowledge has enabled this book. Below is a list of a few scholars whose work has especially been referenced for specific topics that is mentioned in parenthesis. Some I know personally. Most I know through their videos, papers and books. The names are listed alphabetically.

- Ajith Prasad (ceramics)
- Anshumali Bahata Mukhopadhyay (script)
- Arunima Kashyap (food)
- Asko Parpola (art)
- Ayumu Konasukawa (seals)
- Brad Chase (kinship)
- Brett C. Hoffman (bronze)
- Cameron Petrie (climate)
- Daniel Miller (ideology)
- David Reich (genetics)
- Dennys Frenez (seals)
- DP Sharma (art)
- Farzand Masih (Ganweriwala)
- George Possehl (archeology)
- Gregg Jamison (seal and sealing)
- Gyanendra Choubey (genetics)
- Heather Miller (weights)
- Iravatham Mahadevan (script)
- Jeevan Kharakwal (metal)
- Jennifer Bates (food)
- Joan Aruz (fantastic beasts)
- Jonathab Mark Kenoyer (material technology)
- K. Krishnan (ceramics)

- Kuldeep K. Bhan (crafts)
- M. V. Bhaskar (seal art)
- Marta Ameri (diversity)
- Mary A. Davis (veneer)
- Massimo Vidale (heterarchy)
- Mayank Vahia (astronomy)
- Michael Francetti (Pastoralism)
- Michel Danino (measurement)
- Mohammad Rafique Mughal (archeology, Pakistan)
- Monica Smith (textile trade)
- Nisha Yadav (script)
- Peggy Mohan (linguistics)
- Piotr Eltsov (ideology)
- R. Balakrishnan (Dravidian studies)
- Rajesh Rao (script)
- Randall Law (material technology)
- R.S. Bisht (archeology)
- Shail Vyas (music)
- Sharri R. Clark (Ornaments)
- Shereen Ratnakar (geography)
- Sneh Pravinkumar Patel (ceramics)
- S.R. Rao (Lothal)
- Steve Weber (food)
- S.V. Rajesh (Gujarat)
- Vasant Shinde (Rakhigarhi)
- V.N. Prabhakar (beads)
- William R. Belcher (fishing)

Bibliography

- Abraham, Shinu Anna; Gullapalli, Praveena; Raczek, Teresa P; Rizvi, Uzma Z. *Connections and Complexity: New Approaches to the Archaeology of South Asia.* Taylor and Francis. Kindle Edition.
- Ameri, Marta; Costello, Sarah Kielt; Jamison, Gregg; Scott, Sarah Jarmer. *Seals and Sealing in the Ancient World: Case Studies from the Near East, Egypt, the Aegean, and South Asia.* Cambridge University Press. Kindle Edition.
- Ansumali Mukhopadhyay, B. *Ancestral Dravidian languages in Indus Civilization: ultraconserved Dravidian tooth-word reveals deep linguistic ancestry and supports genetics.* Humanit Soc Sci Commun 8, 193 (2021). https://doi.org/10.1057/s41599-021-00868-w
- Ansumali Mukhopadhyay, B. *Semantic scope of Indus inscriptions comprising taxation, trade and craft licensing, commodity control and access control: archaeological and script-internal evidence.* Humanit Soc Sci Commun 10, 972 (2023). https://doi.org/10.1057/s41599-023-02320-7
- Bhaskar, M.V. *Indus zoomorphism and its avatars.* Indian Journal of History of Science. 57, 175–194 (2022). https://doi.org/10.1007/s43539-022-00052-2
- Bisht, R. S., 1997. "Dholavira Excavations: 1990-94" in *Facets of Indian Civilization — Essays in Honour of Prof. B. B. Lal*, ed. J. P. Joshi (New Delhi: Aryan Books International).
- Danino, Michel. 'Dholavira's geometry: A preliminary study.' *Puratattv* 35 (2005): 76-84.
- Dennys Frenez (Editor), Gregg M. Jamison (Editor), Randall W. Law (Editor), Massimo Vidale (Editor), Richard H. Meadow (Editor). *Walking with the Unicorn: Social Organization and Material Culture in Ancient South Asia: Jonathan Mark Kenoyer Felicitation Volume (Orientale Roma).* Archaeopress Archaeology, 2018.
- Farmer, S. *et al.* The Collapse of the Indus-script Thesis: The Myth of a Literate Harappan Civilization. *Electron. J. Vedic Stud.* 11, 19-57 (2004)
- Frenez Dennys (2018) Private Person or Public Persona? Use and Significance of Standard Indus Seals as Markers of Formal Socio-Economic Identities, in D. Frenez, G. M. Jamison, R. W. Law, M.
- Graeber, David; Wengrow, David. *The Dawn of Everything: A New History of Humanity.* Penguin Books Ltd. Kindle Edition.
- Graeber, David. *Debt: The First 5000 Years.* Penguin Books Ltd. Kindle Edition.
- Kenoyer J. Mark (1986) Urban Process in the Indus Tradition: A Preliminary Model from Harappa, in Richard H. Meadow (ed.), Harappa Excavations 1986-1990: A Multidisciplinary Approach to Third Millennium Urbanism (Monographs in World Archaeology No. 3). Madison, WI: Prehistory Press, 29-60.

- Kenoyer, Jonathan Mark. 1998. *Ancient Cities of the Indus Valley Civilization*. Karachi & Islamabad: Oxford University Press & American Institute of Pakistan Studies,
- Lahiri, Nayanjot. *Finding Forgotten Cities: How the Indus Civilization was discovered*. Hachette India. 2012.
- Lal, B. B. 2002. *The Sarasvati Flows On: The Continuity of Indian Culture*. New Delhi: Aryan Books International.
- Miller, Daniel. *Ideology and the Harappan civilization*. Journal of Anthropological Archaeology, Volume 4, Issue 1,1985, Pages 34-71, ISSN 0278-4165. https://doi.org/10.1016/0278-4165(85)90013-3.
- McIntosh, Jane R. *The Ancient Indus Valley: New Perspectives (Understanding Ancient Civilizations)*. ABC-CLIO, 2007
- Nayanjot Lahiri. *The Decline and Fall of the Indus Civilization*. Sangam Books Ltd. Kindle Edition.
- Possehl, Gregory L. *The Indus Civilization: A Contemporary Perspective*. AltaMira Press. Kindle Edition.
- Rao, R. P. N. *et al*. Entropic Evidence for Linguistic Structure in the Indus Script. *Science* 324, 1165 (2009)
- Ratnagar, Shereen. *Understanding Harappa: Civilization in the Greater Indus Valley*. Tulika books, 2015.
- Robinson, Andrew. *The Indus: Lost Civilizations*. Reaktion Books. Kindle Edition.
- Vahia, Mayank N., and Srikumar Menon. *A possible Harappan astronomical observatory at Dholavira*. arXiv preprint arXiv:1310.6474 (2013).
- Vidale Massimo (2010) Aspects of Palace Life at Mohenjo-Daro. South Asian Studies 26, 1: 59-76.
- Vidale Massimo (2018) Heterarchic Powers in the Ancient Indus Cities. Journal of Asian Civilizations 41,2: 1-193
- Vidale, R. H. Meadow (eds.), Walking with The Unicorn: Social Organization and Material Culture in Ancient South Asia. Oxford, UK: Archaeopress, 166-193.
- Wengrow, David. *The Origins of Monsters: Image and Cognition in the First Age of Mechanical Reproduction* (The Rostovtzeff Lectures Book 2). Princeton University Press. Kindle Edition.
- Wengrow, David. *What Makes Civilization?: The Ancient Near East and the Future of the West*. OUP Oxford. Kindle Edition.
- Yadav, N. *et al*. A statistical approach for pattern search in the Indus writing. *Int. J. Dravidian Linguistic* 37, 39 (2008)
- Yadav, N. *et al*. Segmentation of Indus texts. *Int. J. Dravidian Linguistic* 37, 53 (2008)

About the Author

Devdutt Pattanaik writes, illustrates and lectures on the relevance of mythology in modern times. He has, since 1996, written over fifty books and 1,000 columns on how stories, symbols and rituals construct the subjective truth (myths) of ancient and modern cultures around the world. To know more, visit devdutt.com.

HarperCollins *Publishers* India

At HarperCollins India, we believe in telling the best stories and finding the widest readership for our books in every format possible. We started publishing in 1992; a great deal has changed since then, but what has remained constant is the passion with which our authors write their books, the love with which readers receive them, and the sheer joy and excitement that we as publishers feel in being a part of the publishing process.

Over the years, we've had the pleasure of publishing some of the finest writing from the subcontinent and around the world, including several award-winning titles and some of the biggest bestsellers in India's publishing history. But nothing has meant more to us than the fact that millions of people have read the books we published, and that somewhere, a book of ours might have made a difference.

As we look to the future, we go back to that one word— a word which has been a driving force for us all these years.

Read.